Praise for *The Little Things*

"In the first year of our relationship with Andy Andrews, Fairway doubled its business volume—from $5.4 billion to $11.2 billion. Presently, we are ahead of that year's pace by 57 percent. Andy proves what he teaches—that there is unimaginable value in 'the little things' most people overlook."

—STEVE JACOBSON
FOUNDER AND CEO, FAIRWAY INDEPENDENT
MORTGAGE CORPORATION

"I have recommended Andy Andrews to PGA tour members for years. From the Ryder Cup captain to the journeyman pro, Andy notices little things that lower scores, enhancing the games of the best players on the planet. With this, his latest book, he will do the same for your business, your family, and your life."

—GILBERT LITTLE
CEO AND MANAGING PARTNER, UNDER PAR LIFE, INC.

"At Kamado Joe, we understand that it's not enough to have the best grill on the market. There are subtle ways of communicating truth to potential customers that can make them partners in a company's mission. There is one man we've found who can consistently reveal those methods. Since Andy Andrews started working with Kamado Joe, we have increased our sales by 227 percent."

—BOBBY BRENNAN
PRESIDENT AND CEO, KAMADO JOE, INC.

"Are you stuck? Andy Andrews can get to the heart of your challenge faster than any person alive. Then just as quickly, he can deliver an understandable plan of action that will take you from where you are to where you want to be. His written and spoken words have changed the course of my business . . . and my life."

—CINDY MONROE
FOUNDER, PRESIDENT, AND CEO, THIRTY-ONE GIFTS

"Andy Andrews has a reputation for producing results for individuals, families, teams, churches, and corporations. In *The Little Things*, he finally reveals the secret to all those successful outcomes. Check out the chapter on change. It is groundbreaking."

—EMERSON EGGERICHS, PhD
NEW YORK TIMES BESTSELLING AUTHOR, LOVE AND RESPECT SERIES

"I met Andy when at Alabama and he worked with our team. He was also a resource for me at Colorado State. As the new head coach of the Florida Gators, one of the first calls I made was to him. Andy Andrews's words are the first I read when I enter my office and the last I read when I leave—every single day."

—JIM MCELWAIN
HEAD FOOTBALL COACH, UNIVERSITY OF FLORIDA GATORS

"Andy Andrews understands the challenges faced in today's world. His astounding ability to identify tiny yet critical components of a larger picture makes him invaluable to any organization struggling through change in a complex environment."

—LT. GEN. MARSHALL B. "BRAD" WEBB
COMMANDER, AIR FORCE SPECIAL OPERATIONS
COMMAND AND NATO SPECIAL OPERATIONS

"Andy Andrews has a knack for detecting the little things that are the difference between winning and losing. Frankly, it's why Andy has become recognizable to 'football people.' Our officials have studied his material, and coaches listen carefully to what Andy says and direct their players to read his books. As a matter of fact, I keep a personal journal with quotes and passages I first highlighted in *The Noticer*!"

—GREG SANKEY
COMMISSIONER, SOUTHEASTERN CONFERENCE (SEC)

OTHER BOOKS BY ANDY ANDREWS

NOVEL

The Final Summit

The Heart Mender

The Lost Choice

The Noticer

The Noticer Returns

The Traveler's Gift

NONFICTION

How Do You Kill 11 Million People?

The Seven Decisions

The Traveler's Gift Journal

YOUNG ADULT

The Young Traveler's Gift

CHILDREN'S AND GIFT

Baseball, Boys, and Bad Words

The Butterfly Effect

Henry Hodges Needs a Friend

The Kid Who Changed the World

The Perfect Moment

Socks for Christmas

THE LITTLE
THINGS

Why You Really *Should*
Sweat the Small Stuff

ANDY ANDREWS

W PUBLISHING GROUP

AN IMPRINT OF THOMAS NELSON

HarperCollins
PUBLISHERS
——— Since 1817 ———

© 2017 Andy Andrews

Published in Nashville, Tennessee, by W Publishing Group, an imprint of Thomas Nelson.

Thomas Nelson titles may be purchased in bulk for educational, business, fund-raising, or sales promotional use. For information, please e-mail SpecialMarkets@ThomasNelson.com.

Movie quotations in chapter 10 are from Jean Shepherd, Leigh Brown, Bob Clark, *A Christmas Story*, based on Jean Shepherd's novel, *In God We Trust, All Others Pay Cash*, dir. Bob Clark (Metro-Goldwyn Mayer, 1983). Quotes transcribed from samples available on MovieWavs.com.

Library of Congress Control Number: 2016920748

ISBN 978-0-7180-7732-7

Printed in the United States of America

17 18 19 20 21 LSC 6 5 4 3 2 1

To Maryann and Tyler,
I am forever grateful for your influence and example.

Contents

Introduction

> *I am about to take a belief you may have held for*
> *years—a common assumption about what is required*
> *to reach the top of your chosen profession or to live*
> *a successful life—and turn it upside down.*

SOON YOU WILL COME TO UNDERSTAND HOW AND why a simple adjustment in perspective can produce personal and career results far beyond what most people ever imagine.

Interested?

First, allow me to introduce myself. My name is Andy Andrews. I am a Noticer.

It is entirely possible that I am the first *professional* Noticer you've ever met. I'll admit it's an unconventional label, but no other word so perfectly describes what I do. One person may have an amazing voice or is athletically gifted. Another might have a talent for mathematics, fashion, or teaching. Me? I notice things. Or, more to the point, I notice things other people miss.

If you and I are just becoming acquainted, I can imagine

your reaction. "Seriously? You *notice* things? Come on! How do you even make a living?"

I totally understand the question. It was one I asked myself more than once, and for a long time I wondered if I *would* make a living! After all, this Noticer thing was not a skill I developed. It was just something I had (was? am?). Anyway, there was a period in my life when I only noticed things that were funny. At least they were funny enough to enable me to make a living . . . as a comedian.

It's true. For a number of years I worked in Las Vegas, performed on college campuses, went on television talk shows, and toured with some of the biggest names in show business at the time—Kenny Rogers, Cher, Garth Brooks, and others. And, get this: I was Joan Rivers's opening act for two whole years!

It was the Noticer thing that allowed all that to happen. I saw the same daily events everyone else saw. I heard the same words and phrases everyone else heard. And those words and phrases were all used in the same way. But, for some reason, I saw, heard, and perceived something just a little bit different. For instance:

> My mother used to tell me, "Don't play with that stick.
> You'll poke your eye out!" And I'd always think, you can't
> poke your eye out with a stick. You can poke it *in*. . . . To
> poke it out, you'd have to run it up through your nose.

See what I mean?

Somewhere along the way I began to wonder if I could do more for an audience than simply make them laugh. The answer turned out to be yes. In fact, whatever I did to produce comedy from ordinary situations is the same ability I use today to discern subtle differences that can be harnessed by individuals, teams, and corporations to separate themselves dramatically from their industries' averages.

Today, although the most important part of my life is being a husband and a dad, I continue to work with major sports teams, large corporations, parents, churches, communities, the occasional governmental leader, and America's military.

In addition, many of my books—novels as well as nonfiction—are being taught in classrooms with companioned educational curriculums in history, English, reading, and American literature.

When teachers and professors first became interested in the books, no one was more surprised than me. Soon after the inquiries began, however, with the guidance of my longtime business manager and friend, Robert D. Smith, I made a decision about the books and their corresponding curriculums that turned the direction of the whole enterprise 180 degrees— exactly opposite from the industry norms of education and publishing. Robert and I determined that we could and would bear the cost of having the curriculums produced and would provide them to teaching professionals free of charge.

To say the move was unexpected is an understatement. But both of us are products of public education and have personally experienced the needs of teachers and schools desperate to help children learn. Unfortunately, they are often unable to afford material—even the very best material—to supplement the baseline curriculum required by the federal government.

Today, I am thrilled to say, educators have sought out each curriculum—designed for K-5, elementary, middle school, high school, college, and graduate courses—for their classrooms in more than twenty-five hundred school and university systems.

Incidentally, none of this has happened because I'm special in some way. It's happened because, a number of years ago, I intentionally and purposefully chose to *think* differently. I'm going to show you exactly what I mean in the pages that follow and, if you wish, will lead you to some different results of your own.

In case you're wondering, yes, I still write and speak. Daily, via my website, I communicate online with many people around the world. And I am more passionate than ever about my search to notice that thing—*that one tiny thing*—that, when understood and harnessed, allows me to help *YOU* create a life of extraordinary purpose and powerful results. It's less about drive and willpower than it is about a deep understanding of certain principles and *why* they work . . . every time.

Nothing excites me more than a focused search for little things that make big differences. After all, only the smallest essence of a thing can ever reveal its purity and, consequently, the source of its power.

Remember this saying: "Don't sweat the small stuff"? You've

heard it thousands of times, and honestly, on the surface, the admonition appears to be entirely logical. And, without thinking too deeply about this seemingly innocent phrase, we have bought into its meaning wholeheartedly. In fact, our belief in the truth of this statement is so complete that it can now be found by searching the Internet for words like *wisdom* or *proverbs*. Millions of us even bought a book with those words as its title.

Unfortunately, as good as it sounds and as tempting as it may be to follow that instruction, there is a big problem with not sweating the small stuff. Simply said, it's a decidedly unproductive approach to virtually everything in your life you consider important.

If you really expect the results of your life to be any better than the rest of humanity's average, you'd be smart to understand that sometimes . . . conventional wisdom is not even the truth.

Or, in other words, it's time to sweat the small stuff.

There are those who claim to be big-picture people. While their descriptions of future results are often grandiose and exciting, sometimes we elevate these people into leadership positions too quickly. For despite their big dreams, they may have no concept of all the little things that must be factored in, delegated, worked out, and completed in order for the big picture to actually come together.

Yes, it is critical to have a vision. But it is foolish to ignore the fact that every big picture ever completed was created by tiny, almost indiscernible movements of a brush and hand.

One of the greatest "big pictures" in history hangs in the Louvre. When Leonardo da Vinci painted the *Mona Lisa*, he chose to work with the smallest brush he had ever used. The pressure he applied with that brush was so delicate and the movements of its tip so slight that, today, even with a magnifying glass, one cannot discern the individual brushstrokes. Yet they were obviously applied one at a time, carefully, and with loving attention.

Why? Because da Vinci was creating a masterpiece.

What are you creating? To what or whom are you paying close attention as you build your life? However your family turns out, whatever happens with your business, your organization, or your team—at the end of it all, whether you produce a disaster or a masterpiece—it all will have been created one small brushstroke at a time.

So sweat the small stuff.

Seriously.

Author's Note

GOSH, YOU'RE STILL HERE. THAT'S A GOOD SIGN, I SUPpose. I mean, the book is open and in your hands; therefore, the introduction did not prompt you to fling it Frisbee-like through the nearest window. Then again, perhaps you're like me. When it comes to forewords and introductions and prefaces, I rarely even read them.

However—like you, right now—I do read the author's note. Always. I just figure it must contain some little something the author wanted to get across to the reader but forgot to put in the body of his work. Or maybe it was something he learned after the book was written.

I've always figured the decision to include an author's note in a book is like having to drive back to the office because you remembered something you wish you'd told your buddy at lunch. An author's note is akin to a yellow sticky note written at the last minute for a friend. Believe it or not, most authors imagine you reading their books as they write them. (*Oh yeah,* we think. *She will love this part!*) When the manuscript is finished, as unaware as you may be about the relationship, the author feels he has formed one with you. Weird, ain't it?

I know in my case, when I finish a book, you remain on my mind. Yes, it *is* odd, but I miss you. I miss thinking about how you might prefer I phrase a certain passage. Occasionally, I even worry about you a little bit. I sift through parts of the book in my mind and wonder, *Will he understand that? Will she get that reference? Does that passage seem too harsh? Will they want to read this to their kids?*

After several months, the publisher sends the manuscript back for proofing, and fairly often I'll think, *I'm gonna add an author's note to this thing!*

"Why?" the publisher invariably asks.

"Because I have some stuff I want to explain," I'll say. Or "Well, there's a couple of things I want to warn 'em about before they read them."

Most in the book world agree that it is the author's prerogative to pen a communiqué to the reader if he wishes. It is, after all, called an *author's* note. On this point the publisher rarely argues. While I am in a revelatory mood, however, and since this is my personal communiqué to you, allow me to drift outside the lines of literary etiquette and snarkily say that the author's note might just be the only thing a publisher will *not* argue about.

Introductions and forewords are a case in point. If the book is destined for nonfiction, publishers insist on them. And I suppose I understand their reasoning. With fiction, there is a story to grab the reader. There is immediate action that allows a novel to assert, "Do not put me down!" But it's not easy to begin a nonfiction book with an assassination or with multiple explosions. Hence, we have the introduction. It is a publisher's hope that a barely interesting topic will be explained in such a way that the reader might actually continue to read.

It's just that, to me, an introduction seems so darn odd. "Have you written the introduction?" the publisher will ask.

The introduction to what? most authors wonder. *What am I supposed to write? Should I tell them what they are about to read? They already bought the book, you know. Let them read it! You want me to say what I already said but say it in another way? Why? I already explained it as clearly as I could, and that's what is in the book. Do you want me to write a not-as-good version for them to read before they read the good stuff? After they read that, will they still want to read the book?*

Of course, authors want to be on good terms with publishers, so we attempt to do as they ask with a smile. Rarely do they see our eyes roll . . . until their next suggestion, the one put forth as soon as the introduction is completed. "Don't you think," they will ask, "that this book just cries out for a preface? And are you going to find someone to write the foreword, or do you want us to line up a celebrity to do it?"

Once more I have to ask, "What do you expect a celebrity to say? 'Wow, this book is great! Read this book!'? Again, the reader *already has* the book. He is about to read it and might actually do so if we could just *STOP* with all the forewords and introductions and prefaces!"

Sheesh.

Now that I think about it, that's probably why I have skipped many an introduction in my time. I also have passed over several hundred forewords and more than a dump truck load of prefaces. Frankly, they're usually boring. (To my author friends who might be reading this, be assured I am not referring to your books. In fact, I don't personally know any authors who have ever had a boring foreword, preface, or introduction in their books.)

Look, if someone is determined to add anything to the meat of the book—especially before it begins—here's all I'm asking: just don't bore me. I'd rather be shot than bored. So inform me. Entertain me. Make me laugh. Teach me something. Make me mad. Just be interesting.

That said, here is the purpose of my author's note to you: to explain briefly the style in which I have written this book so my publisher can avoid what my grandmother used to call a conniption. (As in, "Calm down. Don't have a conniption here in front of God 'n' ever'body.")

Therefore, the style I have appropriated for this tome, dear reader, is the same style in which you and I would speak audibly were we together in the backyard, drinking iced tea. I will ramble some. I will be smart-alecky at times, and some points will be driven in with a hammer. (Occasionally, we might knock down a wall and hammer the thing in again.) I might make up some words (see *snarkily*), leave sentences incomplete, or make one chapter way longer or way shorter than the others. But I'll tell you this: I'm not gonna bore you.

Boredom is the modern world's greatest predictor of self-delusion, and the twenty-first century's huge population of "readaphobics" is a prime example. In other words, too many people think they don't like to read. They are mistaken. They *do* like to read. They just think that they don't.

In fact, when one considers all the people I have met who label themselves as "a person who doesn't like to read," it is astonishing to note that, within minutes, every single one of them has admitted to me that he or she was mistaken. Interesting, isn't it?

With a big smile on my face, here's what I say: "Oh, come on. I don't even believe that." Laughing, looking around for a second like I think I'm on a hidden camera show, I narrow my eyes suspiciously. "Seriously . . . you're gonna tell me you've never read anything that's made you laugh out loud? You've never read anything that's brought a tear to your eye or put a lump in your throat?"

Pausing only for a beat, I go right back in. "Really? I mean, come on . . . really? You're gonna stand here lookin' in my eyes and tell me you've never read anything that you thought about for the rest of the day? Or that you talked about with the next person you saw?

"Talk to me here. We need to connect with reality . . ." I roll my eyes. Both of us are laughing. "Just answer this," I say. "With a straight face, can you honestly tell me that you have never read an e-mail that blew you away? Or never read an e-mail that was so great you immediately sent it to all your friends?"

By this time even the toughest holdout has to admit to having done everything I mentioned. At that moment, brightening as if an idea has just hit me, I issue the coup de grâce. "Ooh . . . ," I begin, as if it is all becoming clear. "I understand what you're saying. When you say you don't like to read, what you really mean is you don't like to read books that are dull and uninteresting. Amazing. Gee, neither do I!"

At that point, I grin and look 'em right in the eye. Of course, they smile. They know they've been trapped. "Look," I say conspiratorially, "you know I'm a writer. But I'm not saying that you need to read my books. What I *am* saying is that to get what you want in this life you need to read *somebody's* books. Just find somebody who doesn't bore you to tears." And we laugh.

This is the last thing I say: "You know what? I don't just hate reading boring books. I hate being bored, period. Even for a little while. You should try my surefire boredom cure. A lot of times, I just yank a couple of pages out of whatever book I'm reading at the time and shove them into my pocket. When I'm in line at a convenience store, when I'm in a restroom, when I'm waiting on my wife or one of the boys—because I hate being bored and because I hate waiting—I pull that page out of my pocket and read for a little bit.

"Don't be afraid. Just tear the pages out. There's nothing wrong with doing it. It's not like you're ripping up the Bible (even though if tearing a page out meant we'd read what's in it, I'll bet God would give the go-ahead). Look, I figure if I can read something in thirty seconds or a minute that will give me an edge to making more income or having more peace in my family, I'm on it. The alternative is to stand there, be bored, and do nothing. And that is unacceptable."

Boredom is unacceptable for me as a writer, too, so I have deliberately written this book in short bursts. There are stories in it, interesting stories that make a point and have a purpose beyond the point. Some chapters are short, some a bit longer. There are chapters that will make you laugh, a couple that might make you uncomfortable, but all of them, I hope, will prompt you to think differently. There are chapters that will bring peace to your family, and there are a few—pay close attention to these—that, when you harness what they teach, can make you a lot of money or turn your team into a winner.

In any case, I promise you'll find little things on every page that will allow you to make your life the one of your dreams. So go ahead. Yank out a couple of pages and get started!

—Andy Andrews
Orange Beach, Alabama

Preface

HA! I'M JUST KIDDING. THERE'S NOT A PREFACE. TURN the page.

One

A Little Thing . . . *like a one*

> *How many ideas are out there, waiting*
> *patiently for you to show up?*

HOW DOES THAT SONG GO? YOU REMEMBER IT, DON'T
you?

> *One is the loneliest number that you'll ever do . . .*

It's amazing when you think about it. Harry Nilsson wrote
a piece of music about the smallest number in the world. Three
Dog Night recorded it as a *single,* and the song was a huge hit!

Of course, *one* isn't just small and lonely. That number
packs a lot of power. Yes, one. One second, one degree, one idea,
one more . . .

One more? Ah, yeah. That would be *two.* And there's a
canyon of difference between one and two. From 1967 to 1973,
the UCLA men's basketball team under John Wooden won a
remarkable seven national championships in a row. That's right.

Seven consecutive times the team ended the season at number one. Can you name any of the teams that claimed the number two spot?

Who won the last Super Bowl? You remember that, don't you? Quickly now, who did they beat? Odd, isn't it? With thirty-plus teams in the NFL, most of us can't remember the second-best team of less than a year ago!

The modern Olympics have been contested for well over a century and have been the source of many memorable—even legendary—moments for many of us. I wonder . . . how many gold medalists can you name? Now make a list of the silver medalists you can remember. Don't feel bad. I can't name more than a couple either. But that's the point, isn't it? There's a big difference between one and two.

How about one idea? The airplane, penicillin, air conditioning, the computer—before they were physical, workable realities, these examples and a million more life-changing inventions or discoveries were merely ideas. In fact, each was ONE idea. It's an empowering realization. In order to change your life, all YOU need is one idea.

Even in the toughest of times, one idea can save the day. In crisis, most people default to excuses of not having enough money or enough time or lacking leadership.

It is important to remember, however, that you aren't *really* lacking money. You aren't *really* lacking time. Or leadership. You are only lacking one thing. An idea.

One idea will change everything. One idea will change the

world. You and I have seen one idea make billions of dollars. We've seen one idea save millions of lives. And one idea can move you from where you are to where you want to be.

Incidentally, don't ever allow yourself to believe that all the great ideas have been taken. Never forget that, as a society, we put men on the moon before anyone thought to put wheels on luggage!

How many ideas are out there, waiting patiently for *YOU* to show up?

Or consider not just the power of one, but the power of a *fraction* of one. When considering financial reward or future opportunities, is there also a significant gap in those items between first and second place? Of course there is. But how much of a gap?

The financial difference in the opportunities offered to a gold medalist versus a silver medalist is hard to quantify, considering the variety of Olympic sports that are contested. But it is clear. Michael Phelps has had more of life's opportunities, personally and in business, because he has won gold medals instead of winning "only" silver.

Decades after winning gold medals, athletes like Mary Lou Retton, Sugar Ray Leonard, Michelle Kwan, Carl Lewis, Peggy Fleming, and Mike Eruzione are all remembered and revered. They also continue to be well compensated. In fact, many gold medalists are paid tens of thousands of dollars merely to stand in front of a group of people and recount their athletic experiences. The silver medalists . . . not so often.

"Okay," you say. "This is all very obvious. What's the point?"

Well, the point is very simple, but for some reason it is often missed in our almost constant struggle to understand that ever-popular big picture. You see, the point of demonstrating the chasm between first and second place is not to illustrate the financial difference. Or even to show the financial reward produced over time by lasting fame.

No, if you and I are to become extraordinary achievers, we must learn to recognize the little things that actually *create* the gap—and, consequently, the difference in opportunities—between one and two. Astonishingly, these little things that most people see as irrelevant sometimes occur days or even weeks in advance of the event.

And know this: the difference really *is* in little things because the actual gap between first and second place is most often ridiculously small. In fact, as with multiple Olympic sports, the difference between first place and *tenth* place is less than a second.

During one of his many appearances in the Olympic Games, American swimmer Michael Phelps once won a gold medal by a hundredth of a second. Think about it. A hundredth of a second is smaller than the amount of time it takes lightning to strike. It takes more than a hundredth of a second for a hummingbird to flap its wing one time. The blink of an eye takes longer than a hundredth of a second.

Here is the truth that average achievers never bother to consider: the advantage in any arena of life is earned far in advance of the moment one is required to perform. The truth about

Phelps's race is that the tiny burst that propelled him to victory had been acquired in an almost imperceptible manner. It might have been one more swallow of coffee that morning. Or one more practice lap the week before. Or five minutes of additional rest here or there.

Or could it have been a thought?

All activity and movement are initiated in the brain. Had Phelps allowed a negative thought during the race, might that momentary doubt have added two-hundredths of a second to his time? Or was a positive thought, quietly whispered to himself on the starting block, responsible for the hundredth of a second that made the difference between gold and silver?

For winning that particular race, Phelps's former sponsor, Speedo, presented him with a check for one million dollars (which he promptly gave to charity). So whatever Phelps did and whenever he did it, you can be certain that the difference it made was hugely valuable.

And incredibly small.

Two

A Little Thing . . .
like a few nails

> *Be sure you have the details covered.*
> *If you don't take the time now to do it right,*
> *will you have the opportunity later to do it at all?*

HAVE YOU EVER WONDERED WHY THERE ARE OFTEN different versions of a single event that occurred hundreds of years ago? Competing versions of the same story appear frequently when one is exploring the historical record. History is like that, you see. Most people never notice that there is a big difference between "history" and "the past." Simply put, *the past* is what actually happened. *History* is merely what someone wrote.

In a nutshell, the contrast between the two reveals why so many different versions of the same event can be found on the Internet and in history books. It also explains why, when an incident is retold or rewritten, small parts of the story are often ignored or edited out of the final version. Regrettably, these tiny omissions can dramatically change what schoolchildren and society as a whole are able to learn from what *really* happened. A classic case in point is the story of Napoleon's victory at Waterloo.

"Wait a minute," you say. "I thought Napoleon was *defeated* at Waterloo." Of course, you are correct. It is true that Napoleon was beaten badly that day—but only after he won. Here's the story.

In February 1815, Napoleon fled from Elba, where he had been exiled by the allied governments of Europe. This signaled the start of what we now call the Hundred Days Campaign. During this time, not a soul relaxed in the capitals of Europe. They were terrified of Napoleon. Those fears were well founded, for when Napoleon reached Paris, the first move he made was to organize an army for the express purpose of sweeping across the continent.

Many of his former generals were dead or had switched allegiances. Desaix had been killed at Marengo, Lannes at Aspern. Junot shot himself. None of it was of any concern to Napoleon. He believed himself capable of independent command. He was a military genius. After all, everyone told him so.

Amazingly, after several months of campaigning, it appeared Napoleon's view of himself was quite accurate. It wasn't until June 18 that the emperor's situation took a dramatic turn.

That morning, just after daylight, Napoleon was having breakfast with his generals at Rossomme Farm, their temporary headquarters. One of his leaders worried aloud about Wellington's strong position, being situated on high ground at Mont-Saint-Jean.

The emperor scoffed, "It does not matter where Wellington chooses to fight. We have no possibility of defeat!" It certainly appeared that his was a well-reasoned confidence. Napoleon had 72,000 men and 246 cannons compared to Wellington's 67,000 men and 156 cannons.

Napoleon rode a small gray horse and was dressed in a gray topcoat with a dark purple silk vest as he set out that morning. His white trousers covered boots that came just past his knees. As he was about to send his troops into battle, the emperor turned to his next-in-command, Marshal Michel Ney. "If my orders are well executed, we shall sleep in Brussels tonight."

All day long Napoleon sent wave after wave of infantry against Wellington's forces. At the end of the afternoon, Ney and his massed cavalry were ready to finish the battle. These were Napoleon's strongest, most experienced, and most effective fighters—five thousand of them. As the finest horses in Europe stamped with nervous anticipation, the sun shimmered reflections from five thousand swords. Pennants, held aloft on the tips of five thousand lances, fluttered in the wind as the emperor reviewed the situation one last time.

One bold sweep, he knew, would separate the enemy from their cannons; then he would cut them down. *Yes, it would work.* A well-executed cavalry attack would be devastating. And all Napoleon had to do was push Wellington's men away from their cannons. Because of this, he would not separate his divisions, but would attack in a single broad front.

At 4:03 p.m., the French advanced. Supported by artillery,

the French cavalry was in the center of the attack. The riders started at a trot, heading directly for the huge British guns. Almost immediately, the British opened up with loads of canister, firing thousands of round lead balls.

Directing the cavalry, Ney pointed his saber forward to signal, *La Charge!* Without hesitation, five thousand horses broke into full gallop, the ground trembling from the pounding of their hooves. "Vive L'Empereur!" the men screamed as they raced to engage the enemy.

On the other side, Colonel Cornelius Frazier, battalion commander for Wellington, beheld his worst nightmare come true. A shifting, galloping tide of dust and steel was advancing on his position. *They'll roll right over us!* he thought. Napoleon's men were riding two ranks deep, knee to knee, and though they were headed straight for his battalion's deadly fire, how many rounds could his gunners manage?

As the big guns fired, Wellington's canister tore limbs and turned horses inside out. Riders went down, but nothing stopped the charge. Then, at the sound of the bugle, five thousand spear tips lowered, appearing in front of the horses to form a battering ram of pointed steel.

Another blast from the enemy's guns tore into the riders. Every gun, every battery on the hill was blasting away, but nothing stopped the charge of the French cavalry.

Wellington's gunners managed to loosen off one more round of canister as riders and horses piled into them. Less than five minutes later, Ney was out in front, watching as the British gunners dropped their sponge staves and deserted their cannons. The men continued to push and fight until the French infantry had captured every single enemy cannon.

They had done it. Ney and his cavalry had driven the English from their artillery. The French infantry had captured the guns, and Napoleon had defeated Wellington at Waterloo.

It's a great story, isn't it? And absolutely true. What is rarely mentioned, however, is the tiny detail that was ignored that day, leading to a massive reversal of fortune. It was truly a "little thing," but it turned Napoleon's victory into a defeat so devastating that it not only ended the emperor's dominance and reputation but also established the word *Waterloo* as a historical synonym for "a final comeuppance."

At that time, both the French and the English artillery utilized muzzle-loading cannons. They were made of bronze, weighed well over a ton, and were fired by setting a glowing fuse or small flame to a narrow firing touchhole that was drilled through the solid bronze. Traditionally, when troops would overrun an opponent's cannon, headless nails were hammered down into that touchhole, rendering the cannon useless.

On that day, before the battle, several infantry privates had searched in vain for a cask of nails. "Nails!" they called. "We must have nails!" Their confusion was ignored.

As you already know, Napoleon defeated Wellington. He overran the British troops and took possession of their artillery. For several hours the battle raged back and forth until, finally, a group of Wellington's men got their cannons back. Soon another group recaptured theirs. And, suddenly, the British cannons that should have been out of service were being turned back upon the French, firing into them, turning victory into defeat.

Witnesses said Napoleon stood on a hill above the battle, beside his horse, with his hands behind his back. He could do nothing but watch his men—soldiers who had already defeated Wellington's forces—be blasted to pieces.

Nails! Just a few nails, and the British cannons would have been out of action. It was the smallest of elements in a massive clash of men and steel, but had that one detail not been overlooked, history books would now contain the record of a French victory . . . and of Wellington's Waterloo.

Today, the lesson we learn from Napoleon's gaffe is stunning in its combination of simplicity and gravitas. Knowing how well the 72,000 French troops were equipped and provisioned, it is almost inconceivable that a small, overlooked detail could matter so much. But it did. Napoleon's men were the best in the world. On the battlefield that day, they had guns and horses. They had swords and lances and cannons. They just didn't have any nails.

Britain and France. Napoleon and Wellington. The Battle at Waterloo will be remembered forever. It was a clash of nations.

And the whole thing was decided by a fistful of nails.

Three

A Little Thing . . .
like taking offense

> *You can always choose how you*
> *act, despite how you feel.*

NOT TOO LONG AGO, THE CANYONS SCHOOL DISTRICT in Salt Lake County, Utah, built a brand-new high school. By mailed ballots, the board of education allowed the future students of Corner Canyon High School in the town of Draper to vote and choose the new school's mascot. By an overwhelming margin, the students enthusiastically chose "Cougar." The students agreed that, even in a cheer, nothing sounded better than "We are the Cougars! The Cougars! The Corner Canyon Cougars!"

To most, the mascot was not a shocking choice. The cougar has been embraced as a mascot in Utah for quite some time. Brigham Young University in Provo, the fourth-largest employer in the state, selected the cougar as its mascot in 1924, and ever since, the BYU Cougars have been a source of pride. Their academic and philosophical influence is worldwide, and their athletic programs are among the elite, having won ten national championships in five different sports. This includes a football national championship in 1984.

Another reason the mascot choice seemed so appropriate: actual cougars live in actual Utah canyons. In fact, there is a 10,409-acre tract of uninhabited backcountry protected by the Bureau of Land Management. Its official name is "Cougar Canyon Wilderness."

Together, all the facts seem to present an impressive argument for choosing the cougar as a mascot for the new school. But none of that mattered to the Canyons Board of Education. After receiving several calls from presumably horrified people, the superintendent announced the board's refusal to name the cougar as a mascot.

Why?

"Because the word has a derogatory connotation," he explained, "and *might be offensive to older women.*"

Really? Wow!

More and more often these days, the tail is wagging the dog. One person who claims to have been greatly offended is immediately afforded a media platform that is simply unavailable to hundreds of people who are apparently too boring to offer us anything more than common sense.

Even a consensus of leaders who have proven their common sense and value over time are no longer allowed to make decisions without threats and demands from those who claim offense and those who claim they might one day be offended. We hear the loud demands of those who yell, "What I believe is just as valid as anything you or anyone else believes! I will *NOT* be marginalized!"

Many of these people—often simply because they obstruct traffic or interrupt a meeting or pitch a tent in the doorway of someone's business—are invited to share their beliefs on television. Even more incredibly, their behavior often leads to funding by government programs. It is interesting to note how consistently they are treated with tolerance by the very people whose lives they are disrupting.

Perhaps most unsettling of all, however—at least to responsible parents—is an awareness of a dangerous irony awakening in the minds of our children and teenagers. As young people watch adults on television being financially rewarded and becoming famous because of their behavior, our children cannot help but reflect that if *they* acted that way, they would be punished.

Sadly, it is the *wise* voices among us who are being marginalized. By our silence, we allow those voices to be shouted down by fools who rule their own lives (and, increasingly, ours as well) according to the ebb and flow of their emotional tides.

At the root of it all is a misguided belief that "truth" is a malleable concept to be individually defined (and changed) according to how one feels at the moment. Not surprisingly, this cultural march toward relativism and its dictate for absolute tolerance has created in our midst an awful lot of *in*tolerant people. As you might have noticed, intolerant people are easily offended, and offended people often become very, very angry.

This is a societal problem on many fronts. First, offended people often feed on their offense, becoming progressively angrier over time. Then, as we all know, angry people are among our least effective fellow citizens.

Angry people do not make great employees. Angry people do not make great employers either. Angry parents raise angry children. Angry teachers do not inspire or encourage. Angry doctors make mistakes. Angry law enforcement personnel go overboard. Angry teammates attract penalties the whole team must bear.

The uncomfortable truth is this: angry segments of society, no matter how great their numbers, always collapse, crushing the innocent along with the guilty under the weight of their anger.

Final note before we go on: I don't know of any other little thing that wields as much *negative* power as taking offense. That's probably because it affects so many other people. Taking offense begins a "butterfly effect" just like anything else. But on the butterfly responsible for offense repercussions, those evil wings must be the size of a 747!

In case there comes a time when you need to bring a loved one to his or her senses about the damage done by a little thing like taking offense, the following is a dissection in three parts— all on taking offense. If you wish, you have my permission to read it aloud to your family, but I'd do it right away. This is a tough thing to stop when it gets a head of steam. But with a bit of understanding and a commitment to one another—at home and at work—you can avoid it altogether. And if you can, you should.

One

In the scheme of life itself, things don't get much smaller than an offense.

We can *choose* to be offended. We can choose *not* to be offended. It really is that simple. Not necessarily easy. Simple. And always a choice that is completely within our control.

We can *choose* to be upset, hold a grudge, squander time, waste energy, repel opportunity, stagnate professionally, and ruin lifelong relationships because of that choice. Or we can *choose* to grow up, laugh, shrug, forget it, and move on.

We can *choose* not to allow the choices and actions of someone else to dictate our own.

Two

When a person says, "What I believe is just as valid as anything you or anyone else believes," recognize the statement for what it is: a declaration that is not only childish and untrue but also easily refuted. Mature people understand that while they are entitled to their own opinions, they are *not* entitled to their own facts.

While it is true that you are free to believe anything you wish, the rest of us should not be expected—and certainly not compelled—to recognize, respect, or fund foolishness just because *you* believe it. You can believe that trees have feelings. If you choose, you can believe that they dance together or talk to one another. And you may believe it all sincerely. In reality, however, that only makes you sincerely wrong.

That said, please understand that if you *want* to believe that trees talk to one another, fine. Most of us don't care. However, if you assert that, because of *your* belief, *I* can't cut down a tree in my own yard, then *we* have a problem.

Furthermore, if you manage to convince 10 percent of the world's population that trees talk to one another and now, because your group believes it, the rest of us cannot use our own property as we wish, or everyone is required to pay an additional tax on wooden furniture, or lumber companies are prohibited from harvesting timber without your permission . . . I'm sure you see where this kind of thinking can lead a nation of people.

Then again, just to cover the slightest possibility that you don't *get* why this is such a big deal, allow me to grab my sledgehammer and pound this one *all* the way home.

The majority of Americans never even consider threatening anyone, blocking traffic, or disrupting meetings to get their way. The majority are reasonable people. A hallmark of reasonable people is that they tend to assume that most everyone else is reasonable too. Even the tree talkers . . .

Consequently, because the majority of Americans are reasonable and because they assume that the responses and behaviors of everyone else will be reasonable, too, they are very tolerant. Patiently, they project their own expectations of rational behavior and measured responses onto the tree talkers and the misguided or deceived people just like them. And so the reasonable majority—by behaving kindly and tolerating lunacy—unconsciously create a cultural acceptance of a very dangerous fiction: that the emotional beliefs of tree talkers are equal in value to society and to the future of our country as the principled beliefs of the reasonable majority.

This is an oversight with devastating consequences, for *there is no comparative value in the two beliefs.* In this case, an accommodating tolerance from otherwise reasonable people resulted in a collective *decision to do nothing* that had no basis in reality. None. Tragically, this is how a majority of otherwise rational and productive people inadvertently yield their leadership to a small group they quietly believe to be idiots, subsequently enabling the idiots to *steer everyone into a ditch.*

As a postscript to this scenario, don't overlook the fact that the otherwise rational and productive majority are now the ones ultimately to blame for all the damage. Why? Because the majority actually allowed an incredibly intolerant group of people to bully and manipulate them into tolerating decisions and behavior they already knew were wrong.

Three

An offense taken produces a feeling. *Only* a feeling—a moment of emotional confusion. Throughout the course of your life, nothing will prove to be less important. Always remember that you have been created with a will that is stronger than your emotions. You can choose how you act, despite how you feel.

If you are paying the slightest bit of attention, it is clear that we live in a world increasingly obsessed with how people feel. Corporations change policy affecting fifty thousand employees because of how seventeen of them feel. In a country that was founded in part because of a belief in the freedom to worship as one pleases, the freedom to worship as one pleases has been curtailed to protect the feelings of those who might be offended by seeing someone else worship as he or she pleases. Language is carefully policed—a joke can get you fired—and it is becoming increasingly possible to get arrested and not know exactly what you did wrong. Or not agree that you did anything wrong at all.

When you consider the whole attention-to-feelings issue, do you want to know the worst part of it all? Do you want to know the big, offensive-sounding secret no one wants to stand up and say out loud?

It's a lie.

Yep, our whole societal focus on "feelings" as life's most important factor is a dangerous lie. It is a lie that has already greatly damaged the prospects of a generation and threatens to destroy the fabric of our nation.

You see, other than our family or closest friends, and despite laws and regulations designed to protect our feelings, no one really cares how we feel. They may swear that they care. They may have even convinced themselves that they do. But they don't. The bottom-line truth is this: they only care how we act.

This is the way the world has always worked and the way it will continue to work. Don't be discouraged. If you ever believed otherwise, you are about to understand the truth in a way you might never have. You are about to be empowered to create the life of your choosing in a way that will never be possible for those who don't figure this out.

It's not complicated; it's just a fact. Consider our human system of relationships or our nation's economy. Neither one functions—positively or negatively—according to how anyone feels. Quite the opposite is true. Both the economy and relationships are moved only by how we act—what we do.

Again, this shouldn't come as a surprise. Your life has always worked this way. From the time you were a child, not one significant good thing in your life ever happened because of how you felt. All the increases you enjoyed were dividends paid according to how you chose to act.

Think about it. Every boy or girl who liked you, every teacher who gave you the benefit of the doubt, every coach who said, "Congratulations. You made the team"—none of these had anything to do with how you felt.

When you became a teenager, did you ever start a game because your teammates thought it would make you feel good? Did your parents loosen up on the family's rules because you felt bad when you were disciplined? In high school, were you given As because your teachers knew that Cs made you sad?

Then you grew up. Has anything changed? No. To this day, have you ever had a prospective employer stop your interview and ask, "If I give you the job, how are you going to feel?" Of course not. Your acceptance, your opportunities, and your finances are all part of a sliding scale that yields increase or decline according to your body of work. What you do. How you act.

The bottom line is this: when it comes to whether or not you are offended, you are in total control. You can choose to take offense, or you can choose to take action. You can be offended, or you can be cheerful. You can examine your feelings, or you can examine the results of how you have treated people, who you have become, and what has been accomplished in the process.

An offense taken is such a little thing. But when hoarded and fed, an offense is a lot like an actual atomic bomb. The damage it causes—immediately *and* over time—is far, far greater than its initial size would lead you to believe.

﹃ Four ﹄

A Little Thing . . . *like*
a three-letter question

*The distance that exists between how and why
is as vast as the chasm between earth and sky.*

AS CHILDREN, IT WAS ONE OF THE FIRST QUESTIONS WE learned to ask. As parents, it was one of the first questions we begged our children to stop asking.

As children, we were fascinated by how the question could be posed to our parents about anything. As parents, we almost lost our minds because our children posed the question about everything.

The question is "WHY?" It's a small word, to be sure, but the three-letter question has been avoided so often through the years that the reality of its power was lost generations ago. Today, very few people understand the untapped potential available by a deeper understanding of *WHY*.

Years ago there was a television program in which a family

from the mountains struck oil and moved to California. It was called *The Beverly Hillbillies*. The Clampett family lived in a huge mansion that just happened to have a pool table in the main room. The pool table was a source of hilarious conversations because the family had never seen or heard of a pool table. I remember laughing at a scene where the family ate dinner at the pool table and passed food to one another with the cue sticks. They called the cue sticks "pot passers."

I didn't watch the program regularly, so I don't know if Jed and all his kin ever found out the real purpose of the pool table. What they used it for worked for them, of course, and if they never learned any more than what they knew, I'm sure they were happy with that. But you and I know they could have gotten so much more out of that table if they'd only understood how to use it to its fullest potential.

The same can be said about that little word *why*.

There are two angles to the secret about this three-letter word. With an understanding of these two points, you will be able to add fuel to your business and personal life in a way that not only will benefit you financially but also will allow you the opportunity to be hugely valuable to anyone you wish to help.

THE FIRST

The first angle dissecting the secret to why is *WHEN*.

Several years ago I noticed that people struggled and questioned and tried different options right up until the time that whatever they were working on finally came together. When it did come together, they proudly used everything they had learned to keep it all going, but the serious struggle was over. The deep questions, the options, the different scenarios were no longer part of the now-successful enterprise. The gravy train was safely in the station. The search was over.

It all made a certain logical sense, but it bothered me that from that point on there was a definite decline in intensity and excitement. There was no expectation or hope for a breakthrough in methodology or philosophy that might set things on fire again and double the rate of company growth within a year.

When I found the answer, I was astonished by how obvious it was. And it was all a matter of *when*. Here's what I mean:

Question: WHEN do we ask why?

Answer: We ask why when we don't know the answer.

> Examples:
> Why is this not working?
> Why are we not competing well in this region?
> Why didn't our growth meet forecast this quarter?

Question: WHEN do we **stop** asking why?

Answer: We stop asking why when the question has been answered.

Examples:

Everything is under control.

We shifted to a different product emphasis in that area, and that seems to have solved the problem.

We didn't do the customer-appreciation events in July like we usually do.

Are you ready? Here's the big one:

Question: At what point do we RARELY ask why?

Answer: We RARELY ask why when everything is going great!

Let me explain. When things are working, we tend to ride that train until it breaks. When it breaks, we ask why, find the answer, fix it, and ride again.

Why is that a problem? Because it means most of us are missing the best opportunity to learn something that will potentially enable us to grow exponentially.

And how do we take advantage of that opportunity? By asking the question *why* when all is working perfectly! Here's an example:

Statement: We are having great results in the Northeast region. This is the third quarter in a row with a double-digit increase.

Question: *WHY* is this increase happening now? *WHY* only the Northeast? Did you see the charts? *WHY* are the customers making their purchases during lunchtime? And *WHY* are they buying multiples?

If we only ask *why* when something's wrong, the answers we get only take us back to "sea level." But when something really works well, it's not enough to know how it is working. We need an understanding of *WHY* it is working as it is. The answers you receive to the question "*WHY*?" will provide growth like gasoline poured onto a lighted match.

The Second

The second angle to the secret is a corollary to the first. In other words, it's the same, only different!

There are people in this world—we've all seen them—who haven't a clue. They are confused and confusing, and whatever is offered or set before them, they can always manage to screw it up. They are also the only people on the graph who regularly get more than enough sleep. See them? There they are at the bottom. Sleeping! We will represent them with the letter *z*. A lowercase *z*.

z ————————————————————————————————

There is another group of people with whom we are also familiar. And we like them. They are the *D*s. Steady and dependable. Always on time. Whatever comes their way, the *D*s can *do* it. We will bump them up a notch on the graph because, financially, and in every other way that counts, they are higher on the food chain than the *z*s. *D*s make a good living for their families, and they have our respect. So let's hear it for the *D*s!

D _____

z _____

Check the graph now. We are moving up and to the right. See the Ts? The Ts are up a notch from the Ds. They have a higher income level and have a bit more influence in the community. Whatever "it" is, the Ts can *do* it—*and* they can *teach* it!

T ————————————————

D ————————————————

Z ————————————————

Look out! Here come the $\mathcal{L}$s! The $\mathcal{L}$s make even more money. They are also more influential in their communities. Why? Isn't it obvious? That's right. The $\mathcal{L}$s can DO it. They can TEACH it. And the $\mathcal{L}$s can LEAD it. $\mathcal{L}$s thrive on responsibility and are proud of the $\mathcal{D}$s and $\mathcal{T}$s with whom they work. Note that there is a little more distance between $\mathcal{L}$s and $\mathcal{T}$s than between $\mathcal{T}$s and $\mathcal{D}$s. That's probably because of the responsibility the $\mathcal{L}$s take on.

$\mathcal{L}$ ————————

$\mathcal{T}$ ——————————————

$\mathcal{D}$ ———————————————————

$\mathcal{Z}$ ———————————————————

From the Ls on your graph, move to the right and up again, but you'll have to look even higher to find our classic H. Financially and in terms of influence, there's quite a jump from an L to an H. The typical H is the kind of person you and I might label "rich." Yes, they have money and deserve it, having worked hard and created jobs for a lot of people.

Hs are among the coolest people you will meet. They have a ton of influence and are constantly using that influence (and their money) to help other people and to make things better for their communities. You'd better believe Hs can *do* it. It's actually how most of them started in business. Because of their experience, Hs can teach it, too, and often still do. Of course, they can also *lead* it. But here's the kicker—the explanation for their location on our graph—the Hs know HOW it all works!

Because the Hs built their businesses on certain principles, they know HOW those principles work. Consequently, they can build that business again and again in different locations. Ten automobile dealerships, fifteen restaurants, twenty convenience stores—Hs have it happening in a lot of different places. Every time they spot another L, they get it going all over again with a lot of Ds and quite a few Ts, with the L leading the whole thing. Yes, sir, the Hs know HOW it all works.

H

L ————————————————

T ————————————————

D ————————————————

Z ————————————————

There is one more group that most folks know nothing about. They are the *W*s. You won't get to look at them on our graph because they are off the page. Perhaps, if you hold the graph straight out in front of you and look up, the *W* might be on the ceiling. Most likely, however, the *W* is on the roof.

It sounds funny, I know, but this is no joke. These people are so far off the graph that most of their friends don't really have a grasp on what they do. I have found that *what they do* is usually several things, and rarely do those enterprises seem to have any relation to one another.

As I write this, there is a man I continue to think about, a man whose story I know well. Like most *W*s, this man had practical experience. He worked his way from the bottom, first by *doing* it, then by *teaching* it. After a time at this level, he began to *lead*. It wasn't long before he was an experienced *L*, and he began to *teach* another *L* who was less experienced.

At some point during this time, the future *W* became incredibly committed to learning. He continued to work hard, but every spare moment was used studying principles and pushing the limits of what he understood. To his family and friends, he appeared to have become obsessed.

In a way, he often admitted to himself that, at that time, he *was* obsessed. But not with money or cars or even his business. He was consumed by a passion to understand life's principles and how to apply them. He thought often about his friends—the *D*s and *T*s. And he had begun mentoring several *L*s as well.

Looking back, he wasn't certain he could pinpoint the moment when he moved from an L to an H, for he never really stopped to look back. Oh sure, he celebrated his success. And he was able to cut back on his time in the office—what most people called his work. But even when he was home, he continued studying every angle and aspect of the principles he already seemed to know so well.

By then, he was a solid H, and his wife and teenaged children were eagerly joining him in the quest for a deeper understanding of principles. Their lively conversations, filled with laughter, questions, and good-natured disagreements, often lasted for hours.

One day the man had an idea for another business. He didn't need any more money, and he wasn't lacking something to do, but he saw the potential to create more than a thousand jobs in less than two years. With the blessing and participation of his family, the business was launched and began to grow, succeeding almost immediately. The man knew—he *knew*, although he never told anyone the reasons except his wife—that it would not be necessary for him to start at the bottom with *this* company. He had finally begun to unravel a secret that was about to change everything.

As we discussed, the man did not notice when he transitioned from an L to an H, but after several years had passed, he knew that his life was being lived at a different level.

For this telling of his story, I am calling him a W, but he has never had a name for what he has become. Most of his friends have no idea the extent of his holdings.

I can tell you that there are more than thirty companies, mostly very successful, and not a duplicate in the bunch. He has a furniture factory in the American South and a coconut plantation on an island in the Pacific. He bought a failing software company in India and turned it around in less than a year. He owns a factory that manufactures children's clothes in South America and a goat farm in the American Midwest.

Did you know that goat meat is high in protein and the fastest "birth to market" meat produced in America? He does—and a lot more about every one of his businesses. But I don't believe he's completely certain how many of them do more than $100 million in business per year. I heard him questioned about it once. Eight, he thought. Or nine. Or maybe seven. "I'm sorry," he said. "I never really thought about that."

Naturally, magazines want him for interviews. Through the years, all the talk shows have called, but he doesn't want any part of it. Oddly enough, everyone wants to know his secret, and while he doesn't like to sit for interviews, he'll freely give the answer to anyone who asks.

"There's no secret," he says with a polite smile. "In a way, it's all common sense. Of course, principles are the most valuable form of common sense. And they're cheap too." He laughed, adding, "I've never had to pay for a single one, and neither will you."

One day I heard him reveal his secret. It was everything

anyone needed to know about what he or she would have to understand in order to become a W.

The question someone asked was simple, but it opened him up, and it was then that I realized he was anxious to talk. He is a gentleman, however, and he is humble, so he gives the answer only to people who ask.

The lady said, "I love to hear you talk about principles, and I know that you understand HOW all these principles work, but there is more to it than that, isn't there?"

He grinned. "Of course there is. And I don't mind telling exactly what that 'more' entails."

When he said that, those of us who were standing near him didn't breathe. No one wanted to miss what he was about to say.

"This will only take a minute," he started, then cleared his throat. Shrugging, almost as if he were embarrassed that his answer was not more complicated, he said, "Questions are good, and I'm glad you asked this one. All I have done, really, is to hit on a specific question of my own. I apply that question to everything I know. The question is, 'WHY?' That's it. But the answers to that question that I have found over the years have made the difference in my life and businesses. Or let me say it this way: a lot of folks know HOW to harness principles in order to get certain results. Me? I've learned WHY the principles work as they do."

He looked at us and shrugged again. "That's it," he said. "You can know HOW to apply a principle, and that's a mighty good thing. But when you know WHY that certain principle works as it does, you can apply it in contrasting areas of life that seem to have no connection to one another. And those businesses, those communities, those families grow and thrive as never before."

Five

A Little Thing . . . *like*
a sixteenth of an inch

"Almost" can be a dangerous concept. It allows
exclusion, financial loss, even death.
Do not be deceived.
Almost to safety . . . is not safe.
Almost straight . . . is not straight.

EITHER WAY, I WAS BEGINNING TO SUSPECT WE WOULD be dead soon. This would end in tragedy of our own doing. Or Kevin's father, after hearing how stupid we had been, would kill us himself.

How many times had we been told? I didn't want to think about it. I knew it was foolish to run that far offshore without buddies in another boat for safety. But there we were. In one boat. One small boat. One small boat without a large fuel capacity. On the positive side of the ledger, at least a small boat didn't require a licensed captain. So we had certainly saved a lot of money.

I was twenty years old. My right hand had a death grip on the stainless-steel rod holder that was welded to the back of the cockpit seat. My left arm was extended for balance, occasionally waving wildly as if I were riding a bull. Kevin Perkins was mirroring me from five feet away, waving with his right arm.

It would be dark soon. Behind Jim's back, I shot Kevin a worried glance. He and I had been best friends since before either of us could remember and were so closely attuned that often words were an unnecessary impediment to communication. Jim was a guy we'd recently met. He was about our age and seemed an okay sort.

In truth, Jim could have been just released from death row at the state prison, and neither Kevin nor I would have particularly minded. He could have been a foreign spy or a terrorist, and we would have welcomed him into the bond of eternal friendship or blood-brotherhood with all rights and privileges bestowed . . . because Jim's daddy owned a boat.

To this day, our world has rarely witnessed two young men hungrier to fish than Kevin Perkins and Andy Andrews. It is no exaggeration to say that we were well and truly obsessed. There was no hardship we would not endure, no penalty or punishment too feared, no risk dangerous enough to dissuade us from fishing if the opportunity presented itself. And this time, we'd heard the tuna were going nuts a mere hundred miles from our coastline. So here we were.

The wind had increased to at least twelve knots since we left Orange Beach. The seas were running a consistent three to four feet, though Kevin remarked later that he hadn't laid eyes on a wave he thought was as small as three. Adding to the building tension was the fact that, after four hours of pounding along, neither of us had spotted the oil rig that marked the area where we were determined to fish. I saw Jim's head sweep nervously back and forth as he scanned the gray seas. He hadn't found it either.

"Shouldn't we have seen the rig by now?" Kevin yelled over the noise of the twin engines. I looked at my watch and nodded. Jim pulled back the throttles a bit and turned, looking. He didn't say anything. He didn't have to. I saw the fear in his eyes and knew we were in trouble.

For about the tenth time, our new friend leaned down to read the electronics. It was the autopilot he was checking, of course. We'd dialed in the route when the boat left the rocks at Perdido Pass. We had been to the rig before and never thought for a moment that we might have trouble finding it. Heck, it was impossible to miss.

The massive platform was so big that it had taken more than one oil company to fund it. Erected as a joint venture, the rig was slated to pump hundreds of millions of barrels before she was through. Situated in several thousand feet of water, it towered hundreds of feet into the air. From every corner foghorns the size of railroad cars had been attached, each one loud enough to cause hearing damage. As a final touch, the monster had been equipped with thousands of floodlights. It was lit up like God's last bonfire.

Did I mention that you couldn't miss it? Well, apparently we had.

As the sky and water darkened to an inky blackness, the hole in my stomach deepened. The rig was nowhere in sight. In case you've ever wondered about such things, I can assure you very little bravado is left in young men who know they are in deep trouble. And at that moment, we were a pretty quiet crew. Not knowing what to do other than turn around, we did just that.

We were scared and confused. Though it was tempting to declare the rig had sunk or been removed, we knew better. We had friends who had fished it earlier in the week. "Work the west side with ten-ounce diamond jigs," they'd said. "The yellowfins're eatin' the paint off the boat."

Somehow, we realized, we had managed to stray off course. It was the only possible explanation.

Kevin stared at his watch. I didn't ask—I knew what he was doing. He was calculating how long we had run and at what speed. The boat held enough fuel to make it to our destination and back to Orange Beach. *Just* enough. We hadn't planned to troll or try different places. We'd intended to cut the engines and tie to the rig or one of its buoys, drifting live baits and deep jigging.

So not finding the rig at all was alarming. First, of course, because we wouldn't be able to fish. (I told you we were obsessed.) Then there was the possibility that we had somehow passed it and were further out than we had intended. If that were the case, there would not be anywhere near enough fuel for us to make it home.

Jim thought that maybe the rig was shrouded in fog or concealed by clouds. But when darkness closed in completely, we knew that, no, it wasn't even close by. If we'd been within five miles in any direction, we'd have seen the lights.

With no other choice but to head back, we turned into the crossing seas and began to plow slowly—conserving as much fuel as we could—toward land. The wind blew harder. With every minute, we felt the heavy seas relentlessly testing the work of some fiberglass guy who was probably sleeping peacefully in Miami or wherever the boat had been made.

Sometime during the next hour, we did indeed manage a few glimpses of the brightly lit oil rig. It appeared and disappeared several times as a firefly might were it a hundred feet away in a dark brown jar.

The rig was far and to the east of us—where it should *not* have been—but our numb brains barely registered our own questions about how we had missed it by so much. We ground our teeth, concentrated on prayers we hadn't said often enough, and held our breath as the engines struggled through the night on what were quickly becoming only fumes.

When at last the fuel did run dry and the twin motors were silenced, Jim cleated a rope, tied the other end to an empty bucket, and tossed it overboard. Immediately the bow responded to the improvised sea anchor and swung around, pointing the relatively small craft safely into the waves.

We didn't talk, but we were terrified, huddling together as if one of us might hold the key to salvation for the other two. We were cold, wet, and beaten, still wearing the monstrous orange life jackets we had put on sometime in the middle of the night. Though we looked like trick-or-treaters who had gone to war in a car wash, we kept the jackets high and tied tightly. In a sense, I suppose we hoped that when our lifeless bodies were recovered in the days ahead, the presence of colorful flotation attached to our corpses would be evidence that we had at least died with a modicum of common sense.

At dawn, our spirits brightened somewhat with the realization that we were within sight of land. We were saved—but you already knew that must've happened. You are, after all, reading my account of the event. The fact that we were not rescued until later that afternoon lengthens the story a bit, adding several hours of daylight boredom to round out the experience of dark, watery terror the night before. And, of course, the embarrassment of being towed did nothing to add any real value to the tale.

The critical information about our adventure was not discovered until a couple of weeks after our near disaster, when an electronics survey revealed the boat's autopilot was off by two degrees.

Two degrees.

There are 360 separate degrees of bearing in an autopilot's internal compass. Two of those degrees represent a mere smidgen of difference—less than one-sixteenth of an inch—on an actual compass. But distance magnifies the difference.

Most people assume the autopilot is a luxury item, a device that allows the captain to kick back and do nothing. Not true.

Even when the instrument is engaged, a wise skipper maintains concentration, on high alert for any danger ahead. Curiously, the first marine autopilot was installed in 1951 as a fuel-saving device. It's an obvious fact that motoring from point A to point B in a straight line requires less fuel than a meandering route. And in the ocean, with its currents, winds, and waves, there's not a person alive who can look back and forth between freshening seas and a compass while steering a boat and run anything other than a zigzag course.

That day, when we cleared the rock jetties at Perdido Pass, our autopilot was set on a south-southwesterly course bearing at a specifically numbered degree. And it took us on a straight course, as it was designed to do. But the miscalibration meant that the further out to sea we went, the further off course that straight course took us. And we had no idea what was happening.

It's easy to imagine how, in centuries past, sailors thought our planet was flat and feared sailing to the edge and falling over. To anyone headed that far into the Gulf, with no visible point of reference upon which to focus, it always appears as though one is headed into blue shades of nothingness. And so it was that day for Kevin, Jim, and me.

Because of the curvature of the earth, our destination—more than a hundred miles away—was far beyond the horizon. Which was why, at least for the first six or seven miles, we looked back often, as if to assure ourselves that, yes, Orange Beach was still there.

The coastline is easily visible at that distance. Even from

ten miles out, the tops of the high-rise condominiums remain within sight. But the faulty autopilot already had us off course. We just didn't know.

For at least the next ninety miles, we didn't expect to see anything, so we weren't concerned when we did not. We had no way of knowing that we were, in fact, angling farther and farther away from the rig we thought we were running to. By the time our destination should have been in sight, we were so far off course that the rig was hidden beyond the horizon.

Today, when I encounter people who are discouraged with their progress as they start a new endeavor or embark upon a new set of goals, I sense that most of them are attempting to create the big picture all at once. When that big picture doesn't appear as quickly as they had hoped, they allow their imaginations—the part of them that created the excitement in the first place—to turn against them.

Instead of imagining how great everything is going to be and thinking of new methods they can employ to make it so, they imagine all the reasons nothing will *ever* happen. They become discouraged. Ironically, the discouragement affects them physically, and they actually become less likely to do the things crucial to creating the life of their dreams.

And what are the "things" that create the life of our dreams? That's right—small stuff. Small, strategic moves in the beginning of any endeavor yield massive growth down the road.

Your life's compass responds to the same principles and yields the same measure of movement as the compass on a boat. Small moves can equal great gains. In fact, when small moves are repeated consistently over time, you'll one day look up and realize you've traveled all the way from where you were to exactly where you always dreamed you'd be.

❧ Six ❧

A Little Thing . . .
like quitting

> *Yes, everything you do matters.*
> *But everything you don't do matters just as much.*
> *Every little thing you do—or don't do—*
> *steers life onto a slightly different course.*

IT'S HARD TO BELIEVE NOW, BUT THERE WAS A TIME when I hated football. Not all football, though. I loved it on television and the radio. I loved it with the neighborhood kids in someone's backyard. But I was surprised to discover, as a sixth grader playing for our school team, that *real* football was not as fun as it looked.

Oh, it was exciting to think about. Man! When I laced up those shoulder pads and slid my Heard Elementary Rams jersey (number 25) over them, I was fired up. The massive blue and white helmet hung on my head and seemed to hover above a vertical line that usually provoked laughter from anyone near enough to determine that the line was a neck. It was *my* neck.

Yes, I believe myself to have been the original inspiration for the now-popular bobblehead dolls.

After about a week of practice, however, I was pretty sure I wanted to quit. I was prone to headaches anyway, and there was nothing like the combination of high humidity and triple-digit August temperatures in south Alabama to get one cranked up.

"It's only a headache," my father said. "No, you will not quit."

After two weeks of practice I was absolutely certain I wanted to quit. Adding a few hundred laps to the summer heat—with no water (it's how they used to do it)—and staggering along, while the high school kid who was supposed to be our coach channeled Bear Bryant and screamed abuse at me, only added to the intensity of the pain in my noggin. I was not faking. It really hurt—which was why, I suppose, I went crying to my mother. Who told my dad. Who, in his gentle way, gave me two pieces of interesting information: One, I *still* could not quit football. And two, crying would make my headache worse.

Even when the season started, I wanted to quit. It was still hot and humid. Bear Bryant Junior was making us run more and allowing us to drink less. And with the best player in town, Bob Woodall, on my team and available every day to knock my head off in practice, my headaches were developing their own headaches.

But my dad was a rock. Nothing moved him. He was immune to tears, vomit, blood, calculated kindness, fainting, threats of running away, and several manifestations of simulated mental illness. Throughout the season, until the day of the last game, I tried anything and everything I could think of to persuade him to let me quit. But he never did.

I was eighteen years old before I found out how tough that season was on him. It was my mother who told me. She said that my dad had shed more tears that year than I did. He'd shed them in private, of course. But according to Mom, he was determined that I not learn to think of quitting as "just another option on the table when things get tough."

Not long after the conversation with my mom, I asked my dad about that season. I remember my questions, and I remember his answers. But I'm certain I would have listened more carefully if I'd known that within the year my father would be dead.

"I love you so much it hurts," he said that day. "I did then, and I do now. I can promise, son, that I wanted to *let* you quit more than you could've ever wanted to."

"Then why *didn't* you let me?" I asked.

"Because I loved you so much." He paused before continuing. "Quitting a sixth-grade football team is a little thing. And if you were going to be in the sixth grade for the rest of your life, it wouldn't have mattered. But that's not how life works. I knew that you would grow up. As little a thing as quitting can seem in the moment, it moves you in a direction and creates a mind-set that you can begin to see as normal."

I nodded as he added, "And quitting *is* normal for some people. It's *always* easier to quit than to continue on and push through the challenge."

"What if I hit an impossible place?" I asked. "What if there is really no way to succeed at what I'm attempting?"

My dad smiled. "Who gets to decide what's impossible? If you run up against a situation that declares 'there is no way,' then all you have to do is hang in there until you find a way. Get it? You have to find a way . . . where there is no way."

I frowned, and my dad laughed, reaching over to slap me on the shoulder. "Just remember this," he said. "Success takes many forms, and it is on a timetable of its own. You might still think that year of football was a waste or a failure for you. But I'm telling you right now that it was a success. Because you proved to yourself that you can persist through the toughest of times.

"One day—I'm promising this—you will experience a success that happens because of the grit you developed in the autumn of your sixth-grade year. And you'll be the only one who knows the truth about the advantage you had by not developing the habit of quitting."

You know what? My dad was right. Twenty-seven years later I wrote the manuscript for a novel called *The Traveler's Gift*. And no one would publish it.

The manuscript was a story about a man whose family was experiencing the toughest of times. This man, David Ponder, was able to travel back in time to seven different locations. In those places he met with seven historical figures who, at that moment, were experiencing the worst times in their own lives. Each of the seven people gave the man a written principle, and he came to understand that if he made the principles a part of his own life, everything about his future would change.

I thought the book was pretty good. I believed in its message and thought it would help people who were hurting and point them in a positive direction. But the first ten publishers I contacted disagreed. They weren't interested in publishing my novel. Other publishers weren't either. Before long, my number of rejections was up to twenty.

A year went by, then two years. By then, thirty publishing houses had passed on *The Traveler's Gift*. Some of them were quite rude about it.

Did I think about quitting?

Of course.

Would it have been easy to do?

Yes.

Would most people have believed I was justified in quitting had I chosen to do so?

I'm sure.

Fortunately, as it turned out, number seven of those seven principles I had incorporated in the book was haunting me. Every now and then I'd sit in my room alone, turn to that page in the manuscript, and just stare at it. I WILL PERSIST WITHOUT EXCEPTION, it read.

After three years I had received forty-three rejection letters. The letters were from every major and mid-level publisher in the United States. Frankly, I was having a hard time discovering new publishing houses to contact.

I finally hit the fiftieth NO after three and a half years. Then came fifty-one. And by now I had friends telling me to quit.

"Don't be an idiot," I heard. "Don't embarrass yourself like this." One person told me, "Look, you need to face reality and get on with your life. I'm not trying to be unkind here. But, Andy, fifty-one of the biggest, most knowledgeable publishers in the world have agreed that what you have written is not worth putting on paper." Ouch.

Then the fifty-second publisher said yes.

The Traveler's Gift is now available in forty languages and has sold several million copies. More than a decade after its release, it is still in hardcover. It is used by Super Bowl winners, the US military, Fortune 500 companies, and school systems around the world. Churches use it. So do prisons, homeless shelters, rehabilitation facilities, Hollywood stars, Olympic athletes, and several presidents of the United States.

Yes, my father was right about a lot. He was right when he said that quitting was a little thing and not a process with which I wanted to become comfortable. And he was right when he told me that I'd experience a success one day because of the grit I developed in the fall of my sixth-grade year. That particular success turned out to be a *New York Times* bestseller with a direct link to the Heard Elementary Rams. Who could have imagined that?

Seven

A Little Thing . . .
like the other end

> And now, a quick word from your mother:
> *"If everyone else jumped off a cliff,*
> *would you jump off a cliff too?*
> *Just because everyone else is doing*
> *it doesn't mean it's right."*

WHY IS IT THAT WE DO CERTAIN THINGS IN A PARTI-cular way? What prompts millions of us to perform a specific task in exactly the same manner? How can an entire population of people arrive at an identical conclusion about the way something is to be done?

A single result that is common to people the world over? As improbable as it may seem, this is not a rare occurrence. Why does this happen? The simple answer is *logic*. Whether acting individually or as part of a group, you and I overwhelmingly go about our lives—making decisions and performing daily rituals—in ways that, to us, seem most logical.

So, as smart as we believe ourselves to be, isn't it strange to realize that despite overwhelming logic, occasionally our interpretation of the facts is incorrect? That there are actions and methods we have collectively determined to be most productive and about which—collectively—we are wrong? That some of the most obvious things we believe are not even remotely true!

This phenomenon is most easily described with an explanation of what causes it to happen in the first place. Quite simply, we think logically to an incorrect conclusion.

An illustration of this odd but very common occurrence is the way the majority of us peel a banana. The average banana with which we are all familiar is available in almost every supermarket in the world. In Walmart stores it is the number-one item sold. The big-box chain, I discovered, sells more than a billion pounds of bananas every year. Most often it is sold before becoming fully ripened, so the skin of the fruit is usually pale yellow with a greenish cast.

As we all know, every banana has a large end and a small end, and only a quick glance is required to tell the difference between the two. Having done so, almost 100 percent of us grasp the banana at its middle with one hand, using our other hand to open the fruit by peeling it from the large end.

It does seem like such a little thing, but why do we open a banana at the large end? Because *logic* dictates that we must! The proper way to peel a banana has never been disputed. After all, the large end of the banana is where we pick it up. Or hang it. It's the handle! Usually between one and two inches long, the stem is a stable, comfortable, and sizable spot, perfectly suited for a human hand to grab, lift, and peel. "Isn't it plain to see," one might say, "that the large end of the banana was created for this purpose?"

Well, it may be plain to see. But, no, it was not created for this purpose!

This is not to say that the thought process isn't logical. It is. Curiously, without any prior instruction, even a small child will peel his first banana from the large end. So, yes, the thinking *is* logical. The conclusion, however, is absolutely wrong.

Think about it. Have you ever mashed the first part of your banana because the fruit did not peel easily? After tugging and pulling at the "handle," have you ever needed to cut the skin of the banana with a knife or your fingernail in order to peel it?

To be clear, the large end of the banana *was* created for *a* purpose. But that purpose is not as an entry point to the edible fruit inside. Its purpose is to hold up the banana.

When the fruit of a banana tree emerges and begins to grow, it does so in an *upward* direction. That's right. Bananas may *hang* from their stems in your kitchen, but in nature, they do not. A banana grows up.

As a banana becomes larger and heavier, growing in an upward direction, a single stem supports all its weight. Through months of wind and rain, as it endures the stresses of motion and an ever-increasing load, the stem itself grows too. The stem becomes larger, more fibrous, and progressively stronger until, at last, when the banana is harvested, that slender stem has become the toughest, hardest part of the entire banana.

In essence, peeling a banana from the stem is the equivalent of approaching the only door of a house and deciding, instead, to enter from the other side. Through a brick wall.

So the next time you find yourself at the local zoo, make your way to the ape house and take a few moments to observe our world's most enthusiastic consumer of bananas. Watch closely. You'll be amazed to see that, while they lack our powerful skills of logical progression, when faced with the same peeling options as you and me, chimpanzees and orangutans unfailingly ignore what seems so obvious to us and open their bananas from the weakest point—the little end.

Other than being a great conversation starter, does the banana story have any tangible value? To the average person, probably not—except to help us get to our bananas more quickly. But let's imagine for a moment a man named Antonio. Antonio lives in a third-world country and peels bananas for a living.

For years, Antonio has worked as one of thirty or so "peelers" for a small canning operation whose owner pays the workers on a "per banana" basis. He also awards a weekly bonus to the most productive worker, that one person who peels more bananas than anyone else. As they always have, everyone on the crew peels bananas starting at the large end.

About a month ago Antonio had an idea and began to do his job in a manner exactly opposite from this long-established industry standard. Ignoring conventional wisdom and peeling bananas from the other end has allowed Antonio to triple his income. And for four weeks in a row, Antonio has received the bonus for being the most productive banana peeler of them all.

Here is the important part: Yes, Antonio is paid for peeling bananas. But all the money beyond what he was paid previously is, in reality, earned by a function of Antonio's mind and spirit. He used his mind to examine the status quo and recognize a little thing that might make a big difference. His spirit provided the "guts" to try something different, to endure the scoffing of the "experts" with a smile and, thereby, avoid the wasted time and energy of taking offense.

Before we move on, allow me to point out the sad fact that most people live their entire lives without ever thinking beyond what they have come to believe is true. It is a valuable person indeed who manages to see a new way of thinking as an opportunity. It does not matter whether that person is performing a delicate surgical procedure or an everyday, mundane task. By shining a light into the dusty corners of accepted thinking, new possibilities can be discovered, yielding different methods that quite often produce extraordinary—even astonishing—results.

The effects of thinking logically to an incorrect conclusion can be confusing or frustrating. The results of doing so are occasionally funny. Most often, however, when this phenomenon occurs across large groups of people, they are not even aware that it has happened in the first place—then or ever.

When hundreds, thousands, or millions of people basically

agree about how a thing is to be done, you can be sure that "industry standards" have been established. Those standards dictate when the task should be started and the time until completion. As to how long it should be pounded or provided or poured, the proper temperature for maximum production, the time it takes to get up to speed, and the best one can expect—those answers have already been determined. In fact, the outcomes are listed in your best-practices manual.

Because "how it's done" is set in stone, everyone continues to "peel a banana" in the least productive way until someone like Antonio—or you—shows us by his results that a *little* thing can change *every*thing!

Eight

A Little Thing . . . *like an increase in understanding*

> *You can lead a horse to water, but you can't make him think.*

FOR A LONG TIME PLATO WAS "THE MAN." HE WAS A Greek and famous during his lifetime, which was unusual in those days. Four hundred years before the birth of Jesus, if one was not a warrior or government official, it was tough to get noticed. Plato wasn't just noticed; he was revered.

Plato was a thinker. Not *The Thinker*—Auguste Rodin wouldn't create that work of art for another twenty-three hundred years. But Plato was the center point of the philosophical big three. Socrates, Plato, and Aristotle were the acknowledged masters of critical thinking. Plato was a student of Socrates. Aristotle was a student of Plato.

One can only imagine the guts it would have taken to challenge the validity of anything Plato declared to be true. I suppose an ordinary citizen who put himself in that situation would have merely been an object of amused scorn. If one's business were science or philosophy, however, a disagreement with Plato would have been professional suicide.

Enter our hero: Democritus. In philosophical circles he was a minor leaguer to be sure. But Democritus was about to make an attempt to join the big club and break into the starting rotation. And he did it by saying Plato was wrong.

Plato believed that the smallest building blocks of all matter were easily divided into four categories: fire, air, earth, and water. Everyone else (including Aristotle) believed that, too, because that is what Plato thought and what Plato taught.

Democritus disagreed. Democritus proposed that Plato's examples of the foundation of matter could be divided into still smaller parts. To describe the smallest anything could ever be, he offered the word *atomos*, which in Greek means "unable to be cut again." According to Democritus, upon examination, all matter could eventually be reduced to its smallest particle or its atomos. From that smallest point, the matter was unable to be divided again.

The atomos, Democritus asserted, was the building block of all matter. Plato's fire, air, earth, and water, he stated further, were themselves made up of atomos.

As one might expect, when the news of Democritus's claim reached Plato, the fire, air, earth, and water hit the fan. He was outraged, denouncing Democritus in every public forum available (which might have included *the* forum) and advising the populace to burn the upstart's books. For Democritus, this was probably worse than not making the team.

Apparently, everyone did exactly what Plato suggested and destroyed the material that had so offended the great thinker. For though Democritus continued his work, refining the idea of atomos, his writings did not survive. In fact, were it not for references to his work in quotations from other writers, we would not even know the man existed.

Poor Plato. If only you and I could have been there to tell him the truth. Not the truth about Democritus. No, you and I could have changed everything for Plato by revealing to him the truth about continuing to push the boundaries of what we think we know. But Plato handcuffed himself to what he had decided.

How much more could he have untangled and understood if he'd only known that *ONLY A FOOL BELIEVES EVERYTHING HE THINKS.*

Of course, the admonition applies to Democritus as well. Yes, he was correct in his understanding that matter is made up of atoms. However, he was *incorrect* in thinking that his atomos was the smallest form of matter. And he was *really* off base when he named his discovery with a word that means "unable to be cut again"—because scientists have been proving the atom *is* able to be cut again ever since. Irony, anyone?

Poor Democritus. If only you and I had been there to tell him that ONLY A FOOL BELIEVES EVERYTHING HE THINKS.

Here is what we know as of now: Atoms come in at least 109 sizes or weights. Just as every word in this book is created with only twenty-six letters, everything in the universe is made of atoms. They are a basic building block of all matter. And all 109 sizes or weights of them are tiny. In fact, it would take more than ten million atoms, arranged in a straight line across the period at the end of this sentence, to stretch from one side of the period to the other. Did you know that there are more densely packed atoms in your kitchen toaster than there are grains of sand on all the beaches of the world?

But tiny as they are, atoms are made up of even tinier particles called electrons, protons, and neutrons. The number of these particles in each atom determines which of the 109 it actually is. The number of protons in the atom determines what's known as its atomic number. (Note: We won't discuss chemical elements at this time. After all, you memorized the periodic table in high school, and I'm sure you remember every symbol!)

Have you heard about quarks? Scientists have now reduced Democritus's atom well past protons, neutrons, and electrons. They've identified six varieties of quarks mixed in with what physicists refer to as a particle zoo. There, separate groups of particles are called tribes. A quark is a thousand times smaller than the nucleus of an atom. And that's really saying something because 99 percent of an atom is just empty space.

Let's stop here. Yes, we could move into a discussion of dark matter and a smaller division of the particle zoo now being addressed as part of what is called string theory. But for most of us the point should be clear. While others inevitably arrive at the finish line of learning and become satisfied with what they know and who they are, you and I must press on to fulfill the potential with which we have been created.

Don't always believe everything you think. To do so will be the end of any exponential growth you might have experienced in your life.

King Solomon wrote that, throughout our lives, we should seek wisdom as if searching for a lost treasure. He asserted that wisdom is worth any price one has to pay. Truth is the basis for wisdom. And a principle, as you know, is a foundational truth. Therefore, knowing that a foundational truth is always true, it stands that principles always work.

This tells us that if we want to be wise, we should seek to obtain a vast knowledge of principles. We should strive to understand those principles. Then we should dig in even more, thinking our way to a *deeper* understanding of principles.

A deep understanding of principles contains an amazing amount of power and protection for you and your family. Since principles work every time, they work whether you know them or not. Have you heard the phrase "ignorance of the law is no excuse"? Well, remember this one too: ignorance of a principle is no protection from the consequences of violating that principle just because you didn't know it.

Gravity is a principle. It does not matter if you know it, understand it, or agree with it. If you stumble over the edge of a cliff, the principle of gravity will display its full power despite your surprise.

Never forget that gravity was working long before the apple

ever fell on Newton's head. But when it *did* fall and Newton understood what it meant, he was able to explain it to everyone else. Over the years a deeper understanding of gravity was gained. This allowed society to harness that principle and create airline flights, suspension bridges, and any number of things over which gravity holds sway.

A deeper understanding is only *a little more* understanding than you have today.

A little more understanding can change the world.

It almost goes without saying: there is benefit to learning something new. Most interesting, however, is another rarely considered piece of the puzzle. There is a tremendous—almost overwhelming—competitive advantage to be gained in acquiring deeper understanding and greater clarity, learning more about a subject in which you previously did not excel. Or about which you were singularly uninformed. Or dramatically *mis*informed.

Think about it. With perspective and clarity comes the realization that *you now understand something in a way and at a level you could not have previously comprehended it.* For instance, by reading this book, you may now have a different perspective and an enhanced level of clarity about several things that almost none of your competition understands. If you are in business (and if you have a job, you are in business) or if you participate in a sport by playing or coaching, you will begin to master the first stage of a key process I teach my clients: *competing on a level where your competition does not even know there's a game.*

That's easier to do than you might think, especially because the competitors in every industry compete in exactly the same way. And because they all compete in the same way, they watch one another closely and *do what they already know to do.*

In other words, the competition does what they *think* they should do—because of their industry standards, their best-practices manuals, and an embedded cultural mind-set about how things are done.

How will you begin to compete at a different level? By examining your thinking—especially about how things are done in your industry—and realizing you can't always believe everything you think!

So before moving on, here are two significant questions you must face:

1. How long are you willing to wait to change virtually every result you've ever had?
2. When is NOW a good time to begin?

A Little Thing . . .
like perspective

> *Perspective is the only thing consistently*
> *more valuable than the answer itself.*

OVER THE YEARS, I HAVE BECOME EXCITED MORE CON-
sistently about the power of perspective than about any other
principle I have endeavored to understand. Because I am always
learning more about this amazing force, it seems to end up in
every book I write and every speech I deliver—whether it takes
the form of a discussion between characters in a novel or a statement of several facts as I am about to do here.

FACT: YOU CHOOSE YOUR PERSPECTIVE.

*In a world where so many feel powerless, wouldn't it be
great to be in control?* Well, you are—or you can be—if you

understand the nature of perspective and are willing to harness its authority.

Your perspective is yours alone. You own it. No one can change it or diminish it without your permission. You were created with free will. YOU can CHOOSE how you see things. While others see a certain circumstance as the end of the road, you can decide it is only the beginning.

You have no doubt heard that one's perception is one's reality, and that is often true. However, if you intend to live a life of great influence and rich reward, it is critical that you understand the difference between perception and perspective.

Perception—how a situation is *perceived*—has to do with what one decides the facts really are at a given moment. Perspective, on the other hand, has to do with what one decides the facts of that moment *mean* in terms of direction toward one's ultimate desired destination.

Perception concerns what is.

Perspective concerns our ability to direct what happens from that point forward *according to our interpretation of what is.*

Perception can provide an accurate understanding of a particular event in a specific moment, but by itself—used without proper perspective—it can lead to cynicism and hopelessness. Only by adding proper perspective to our perception of a certain situation can we begin to effectively shape the future of our choosing. This is, in fact, the very reason your perception and your perspective about something should almost never be the same.

For example, suppose you perceive a situation as "the worst thing that could have possibly happened." If you allow your perspective to match that perception, you also allow it to determine (and limit) your future. Therefore, and not surprisingly, by collapsing, complaining, and doing nothing, you allow your perception to maintain its accuracy forever. In effect, your perception was right on target, and without the power of a different perspective, the situation really *was* the worst thing that could have happened.

Of course, when the worst does happen, you are also free to choose a *different* perspective. You can choose to get up, shake it off, and smile. You can choose to mine the "disaster rubble" for valuable lessons. You can choose to change gears and start fresh, utilizing different methods, while choosing to be grateful for the rare opportunity to know in advance what does not work if the situation ever presents itself again. You can use extra time to read, to pray, and to be quiet and think. Then you can allow all the new understanding you have gained to coalesce into plans of certainty for an astonishing future you otherwise would have never known.

At that point, you realize that choosing your perspective allowed you to be the author of your own reality. And what is that reality? That *the worst thing that could have happened has now become* THE BEST *thing that could have happened.*

Choosing your perspective will also help you see the difference between what will work and what is THE BEST. One of the most valuable lessons you can possibly learn is that those two are rarely the same. In a time of crisis most people are so desperate for an answer that they will shove *any* answer into the situation without proper regard for its timing or value.

Choices and decisions made by intelligent people will usually work in some way and to some degree. THE BEST answers in a situation, however, often contain an element of timing.

In addition, I would urge you to notice how often intelligent people assemble facts and then make their decisions based on those facts. Actually, it's what most people do because it produces results that work (in some way and to some degree).

Contrast that method with how *wise* people deal with the same types of situations. You'll quickly notice that they also assemble the facts. But instead of making a decision based solely on the facts, wise people first break down those facts and apply a healthy dose of perspective. That perspective allows them to choose THE BEST course of action and set everything in motion at the *very best* time. (Note: you'll find more about choosing THE BEST in chapter 14.)

Perspective about a situation creates calm. Calm leads to clear thinking. Clear thinking yields ideas and helps one discern the difference between problem areas and opportunities. Clear thinking also pinpoints perfect timing. And all of this leads to the answer you will be confident is THE BEST.

FACT: PERSPECTIVE IS THE ONLY THING THAT CAN DRAMATICALLY CHANGE THE RESULTS WITHOUT CHANGING ANY OF THE FACTS.

I could fill this book with stories proving this point. These stories range from individual perspectives that changed career results, to student perspectives that changed grades, to national perspectives that changed history. For our purposes here, let's go for a simple but amazing result produced by perspective alone.

As of this writing, the average fast-food restaurant in America grosses $800,000 per year. And according to the data I found, Sunday is the best day to own a fast-food operation. More money by far is spent at fast-food restaurants on Sunday than on any other day. Pages and pages of data show that this is not a new quirk in America's dining habits, but has long been the case.

For years, every operation in the fast-food industry has had access to the same data, the same facts. After a careful examination of those facts, do all operations see them the same way? Based on the same data, do they all choose the same perspective? No, they do not.

McDonald's looks at the facts and determines that it only makes sense to strike while the iron is hot, to make hay while the sun shines. There is obviously more money to be made on Sunday than on any other day of the week. The increased crowds of customers must be served quickly. Therefore, the McDonald's perspective is that Sunday is a great day to bring in as many employees as possible in order to staff their restaurants with the week's highest number of workers.

Chick-fil-A has also had access to the same data for years. Every time industry facts and figures are released, the executives at Chick-fil-A examine the same details, delivered in the same way and at the same time, as their counterparts at McDonald's. The information is clear and consistent. Sunday continues to lead every other day of the week in revenue by a large margin.

So after examining the same data, Chick-fil-A's perspective is that there are some things more important than merely selling another chicken sandwich. Their perspective is that Sunday is a great day to give their employees the day off. This is done to allow families to be together, to allow a time to regroup and take a deep breath, and to allow their employees the opportunity to attend church if they wish.

Same industry. Same data. Different perspectives. But here is where it gets really interesting. Remember the fast-food industry average? Across the board, all franchises and chains taken as a whole, each restaurant averages an $800,000 gross profit per year. McDonald's operation is obviously way above average, so it probably doesn't surprise you to hear that the average McDonald's restaurant takes in $2.6 million per year.

One might be tempted to think that Chick-fil-A would be overwhelmed by that kind of competition and those kinds of numbers. Not even close. Now remember, Chick-fil-A is never open twenty-four hours a day and never open on a Sunday. Yet with a reduced amount of hours and fifty-two fewer days on the calendar, the average Chick-fil-A restaurant brings in four million dollars per year.

Perspective is such a little thing, but it's the *only* thing that can dramatically change the results without changing any of the facts.

A Little Thing...
like an air rifle

> *In his hand was the knurled stock of*
> *as coolly deadly-looking a piece of*
> *weaponry as ever I had laid eyes on.*
> —JEAN SHEPHERD

THE LAND MASS NOW OCCUPIED BY THE UNITED
States of America was once separated into four parts by casual
borders and owned by four different countries—England,
France, Spain, and a very young United States. This fact, I am
fairly certain, you already know.

There is, however, a footnote to the larger story—one virtually overlooked by historians—about how the youngest country
came to own it all. The tale concerns a two-year period, from
1804 to 1806, and a single iconic gun that was never even fired
at a person. Yet it was used again and again, becoming one of the
most influential weapons in history. There is no doubt that this

one gun—on multiple occasions—bore much of the responsibility for America's expansion into its current geographical form.

Care to guess what kind of gun it was? The Kentucky long rifle, you say? Perhaps your vote would go to Samuel Colt's six-shooter. Anyone for the Winchester lever-action repeating rifle?

No, no, and no.

Good guesses all. But those are not even close to being the gun that enabled the United States to stretch from "sea to shining sea."

That gun was the air rifle.

Intriguing, isn't it? After all, what's the first thing that pops into your mind when you read the words *air rifle*? If your brain immediately conjures up scenes from the movie *A Christmas Story*, you are not alone: *An air rifle? You mean "an official Red Ryder carbine-action, two-hundred-shot range model." The one "with a compass in the stock and this thing which tells time."*

Most people consider the lowly air rifle to be little more than a toy—the kind of present a nine-year-old would long for. But as I stated, there is a tale of power in its past. Real power. The kind of power that can forge nations.

In other words, more power than you'd ever need to "shoot your eye out"!

In May 1804, the Corps of Discovery set off from Missouri headed for parts unknown. Totaling thirty-three men in their "permanent party," they had been commissioned by the third president of the United States, Thomas Jefferson, to "find whatever is out there." Missouri was the country's western edge at the time, and most Americans (including Congress) were of the opinion that whatever *was* out there, the French, Spanish, and British could darn well have it. Jefferson disagreed.

The president had chosen a US Army captain, Meriwether Lewis, to head the expedition. Lewis then selected his friend William Clark as second in command. The officially stated purpose of the journey was to discover a water route to the Pacific Ocean, and Jefferson's public justification for the effort was based on the possibility of greater commerce. Privately, however, he had different reasons altogether.

Jefferson had heard stories of the vast lands to the west. In addition, he had read Captain James Cook's account of his third voyage across the Pacific and the Alexander Mackenzie book, *Voyages from Montreal*, which had been published in 1801. Mackenzie's book in particular convinced the president that England intended to control the increasingly valuable fur trade of the Pacific Northwest. With that information added to the stories of timber, gold, pure water, and fertile valleys, Jefferson decided that America must secure the territory for itself as soon as possible.

Congress would agree to provide only twenty-five hundred dollars to fund the expedition. Almost fifty thousand more was provided by what was described as "Jefferson's secret sources." This money was used to purchase supplies enough to last the duration of the mission—a trip that would ultimately stretch on for two years, four months, and ten days.

The journey began at Camp Dubois on the Mississippi

River north of Saint Louis. On May 24, the men passed through Daniel Boone's settlement. Almost two weeks later, they marked Independence Day in Atchison, Kansas. And on July 21, 1804, the Corps of Discovery reached the Platte River, 640 miles from St. Louis. They had entered Sioux territory.

From that day, what has come to be known as the Lewis and Clark Expedition was in constant contact with Indian nations— the Oto tribe, the Missouris, the Yanktons . . . and none were happy with the presence of white men. In late September, they were stopped by hostile Lakota Sioux. On October 8, Lewis and his men faced off with an Arikara tribe that numbered more than two thousand.

On they went, however, without losing men or supplies— despite constant encounters with Mandan, Hidatsa, Shoshone, Flathead, Nez Perce, Chinook, and Blackfoot.

On November 20, 1805, the Corps of Discovery finally waded into the Pacific Ocean. They decided to winter on the south side of the Columbia River. On March 22, 1806, the expedition headed east and toward home, navigating by a different route. On this return journey, they encountered more and different Indian tribes—almost constantly. They traveled through the spring and summer, finally reaching Saint Louis on September 23.

Two years. Four months. Ten days. During that time, one of their party died of a ruptured appendix. But other than the unfortunate Charles Floyd, Lewis and Clark did not lose another man. To be clear, not a single member of the expedition was lost to violence, despite traveling openly through the heart of Indian lands.

For years, historians have wondered, aloud and in print, how Lewis and Clark could have possibly made it all the way across the continent and back with only thirty men and not lose a life or any supplies to Indians who were openly hostile to their presence. How could they have stood down two thousand Arikara? When Lewis's dog was stolen, how could he have successfully demanded its return? Why would the Shoshone have allowed the expedition twenty-nine horses so they could cross the Rocky Mountains?

The answer to all these questions is: Lewis had an air rifle.

By 1804, the westward migration had made it as far as the Mississippi River. Civilization had pushed all the way from the Atlantic Ocean in a bit more than 150 years. That was enough time and distance to convince the Indians that the white man not only intended to stay but would continue to push the western boundary.

No longer as tolerant to the presence of the settlers or amenable to negotiation with their government, the Indians were determined to defend what they saw as their land.

The fighting techniques they developed to do so were sound. Though, for the most part, they did not possess guns, the Indians did have bows, knives, clubs, horses . . . and an unerring ability to discern the exact moment to successfully attack. Oddly enough, it was the white man's gun that signaled that proper time.

Rifles in the early 1800s were exclusively muzzle-loading, single-shot weapons that took thirty to forty seconds for the average man to reload after they had been fired. The Indians knew this, of course, and would dodge through trees on foot or gallop horses close to their enemies, often hanging from the opposite side of the animals. The point of the tactic was to draw enemy fire. When, inevitably, the white man did fire his one shot, the Indians would immediately rush to attack before the rifleman could reload.

While it is true that an Indian was no match for a white man with a loaded rifle, once that rifle was discharged, the advantage swung the other way. No white man was a match for a swarm of Indians armed with knives and clubs. At close-in combat— hand to hand—the Indian had no peer.

Enter the Girandoni air rifle. Designed by an Italian inventor, the Girandoni was in use by the Austrian Army from 1780 until 1815. The rifle was four feet long and weighed about ten pounds—almost exactly the size and shape of the single-shot muzzle loaders of that time. Its stock was a detachable air reservoir filled by a hand pump that resembled today's bicycle pumps.

The air rifle was beautifully detailed and fired a .46 caliber lead ball that was effective to 125 yards. Because it did not use propellants or powder of any kind, the gun issued no smoke when fired. And because its source of power was simply compressed air, the rifle was strangely quiet, especially compared to other guns of its day.

Yes, the Girandoni was unusual in every way, but its greatest difference was so shocking to behold that it provided the Corps of Discovery a supreme advantage. Snugged against its barrel, the air rifle had a tubular, gravity-fed magazine with a capacity of twenty .46 caliber balls. Without re-pressurizing between shots, the Girandoni could fire repeatedly. When the trigger was pulled, the only move required to reload was a small lift of the barrel. This caused a new lead ball to roll into place, and within seconds the rifle could be fired again.

Lewis bought the rifle on a whim at Harper's Ferry, West Virginia, while purchasing supplies for the expedition. Its addition turned out to be fortuitous. Though surprised at first by the boldness of the Indians, the men soon realized they were being "sized up" for attack. Knowing they were no match for the number of warriors the tribes boasted, Lewis devised a bluff.

Thereafter, immediately upon making contact with Indians—whether a roaming group or a large tribe—Lewis would give the leaders gifts and announce a demonstration. With the air rifle in his hands, he would direct a man to place a target about a hundred yards away. When everyone's attention was on him, Lewis would fire and hit the target . . . again and again and again.

What kind of magic is this? the Indians must have wondered. *The rifle makes no sound and shoots without reloading!*

For more than two years, Lewis's demonstrations protected the party from attack. Interestingly, however, what the Indians did *not* know was as important to the expedition's successful outcome as what they did know.

For instance, Lewis never allowed the Indians to see the rifle being pressurized with air, so they never knew the source of the gun's power—or its limitations. They were unaware that the Girandoni required approximately fifteen hundred strokes of the hand pump to fill the air chamber. And because Lewis always declined to shoot more than twelve or fourteen times in a row for any particular group, they had no concept of how many shots could be fired and simply assumed there was no limit.

Most daring of all, however, was the belief imposed upon the Indians that every Corps of Discovery rifle on the expedition was just like the one used in the demonstrations by Lewis. And so, because the Indians could not imagine surviving against the rate of fire promised by thirty of these weapons, they never attacked at all.

It is an accepted fact among historians that America's geographic reality was made possible by Lewis, Clark, and their Corps of Discovery. Had the expedition failed, had they been prevented from completing their mission to "find whatever is out there," we would most certainly live in a different world today. And to think it all balanced on such a little thing.

Throughout history, the Lewis and Clark Expedition is the only instance on record where an entire nation of people— loosely gathered though they were—was defeated in such a way. Incredibly, the Indians were beaten by an air rifle.

And it was only *one* air rifle.

An air rifle that was never even pointed in their direction!

A Little Thing . . .
like being different

> *Comfort, acceptance, and assurance are life's rewards that the average person demands immediately. The extraordinary achiever, however, chooses to work without any of them for a time in order that his family might enjoy vast helpings of all three for generations.*

WITH SO MANY GOOD, HARDWORKING PEOPLE WHO are striving to achieve more, have you ever wondered why relatively few realize—truly realize—extraordinary results? I believe a large part of the reason can be explained this way: everybody wants to make a difference, but nobody is willing to be different.

If you look closely, you'll see that most of us reach and maintain a level of "average excellence" that aligns rather closely to the achievements of our peers. In other words, we all tend to get the same general results. And not just similar results to those in our office or on our team . . . no, this phenomenon of similar results occurs worldwide in every industry. It is common in all sports, educational systems, and cultural institutions.

In case you didn't already know, average people compare themselves to other people. That is, in fact, why they are average. Other people's finances, marriages, children, houses, vacations, automobiles, you name it—all of these are used by average people to gauge whether their own results are on par. If the average man determines he is a little ahead of his peers, he feels justified in relaxing a bit. If the average woman determines she is somewhat behind, she works harder to catch up. All this happens because average people compare themselves to other people.

In their defense, the vast majority of the things these people overlook are tiny, seemingly ordinary components of everyday life. Further, most folks wouldn't give these things a second thought if they *did* notice them. It's not that these tiny things are not *worth* a second thought. It's that most folks don't *think* they are worth a second thought.

On the other end of the spectrum, extraordinary achievers do not compare themselves to other people. Instead, they compare themselves to their own potential. And what might their *potential* be? Whatever they choose to think it is!

One thing is certain: they will not allow you or me to define it for them.

When I talk to people who work with teenagers, I often ask, "What's the biggest concern teens have in their lives? What do they think about most often?" Their answers almost always have something to do with the overwhelming desire teens have to be accepted or fit in with their peers. There's nothing a teenager hates more than feeling different or "weird." And that's not surprising. Most adults are still dealing with those same feelings.

The following are a few great questions to ask the teenagers in your life. They are great questions to ask yourself as well. Remember, what you're always after is a consistent increase in your level of understanding.

1. When you look around at the way average people live—in terms of finances, time to do what they enjoy, being happy with their jobs or families or businesses—do you think they live exceptionally well?
2. Ten years from now, would you be thrilled to live like the people we just discussed?
3. Why do you think most of them are where they are?
4. Is the following statement true or false? *Knowing that every physician in America graduated from medical school, if a person desires to be a physician someday, he or she had better enroll in medical school.*
5. True or false: *if a person desires to be an attorney someday, he or she had better enroll in medical school.*
6. Why was the answer to the previous question false?
7. Look back at question number two. Ten years from now, if, in fact, you would *not* be thrilled to live like everyone else, would it make sense that the more different you are from them during the next ten years, the more likely you are to end up in a different place?

In most cases, extraordinary achievers became comfortable with being seen as "different" or even "odd" long before they achieved the level of success they were after. It's a distinction that average people often fail to make. If one desires to live life on a different level, that destination will not be reached by traveling the same road everyone else has chosen.

In other words, if you want to be different, you're going to have to be different!

You will need to act differently as well. For instance, in our world today exceptional manners are *different*. And while we are on the topic, it is important to understand that different may seem weird at first, even when it's not.

When I travel, I often give books to people I meet. Once, some years ago, my sons, Austin and Adam, were with me on a trip. Before we left home, I packed several copies of my children's book, *The Kid Who Changed the World*, for each of them. I suggested they might give them away to children and parents we encountered along the way. Unenthusiastically (I noticed), they agreed to do so.

But they didn't do it. As we unpacked after the last leg of the journey, I saw that every book I had given the boys was still in their backpacks. Later, I asked why they had not given a single one away.

"Dad . . . really?" my oldest answered. "We can't just go up to somebody in an airport and give their kid a book."

"Why not?" I asked.

"Dad . . . ," Austin said, as if I should know the answer,

"because it's weird."

I looked at Adam. He raised an eyebrow and nodded, concurring with his big brother.

"Let me be sure I have this straight," I said. "You see a six- or seven-year-old kid with his parents. You approach, smiling, and tell them you noticed the family and have a book for the child. You hand them a brand-new, very colorful, hardback book that has been signed by the author. They thank you profusely, and you walk away." I paused, then asked, "And that is weird?"

"Yes, sir," they both said. "It is."

I took a breath and smiled. "Okay," I said. "This'll only take a second. You want to know the truth, don't you?"

"Yes, sir," they replied cautiously.

"All right. The truth is this: It's not weird. You only *think* it's weird. The reason you think that giving a book to a family is weird is because no one ever does that. But it is not weird. It's different.

"Now, I'll admit that if you ran up to that family, stuck your tongue out, and threw the book at them—yeah, that would be weird. But giving of yourself, being kind, being generous, smiling while you talk, standing when your mother comes to the table, shaking hands when you meet someone—these things are not weird, and don't ever let anyone make you feel like they are. They are different, yes. And should you choose to pay attention to learning how to behave in these ways, your lives will be different as well."

In closing this chapter, allow me to point out that, as a

percentage of our world's population, there are not many extraordinary achievers. That's why extraordinary achievers are considered to be different. Their financial situations are different from those of the average person. They possess different levels of influence. They live different lives.

If you want to be an extraordinary achiever, then you really do want to be different!

A Little Thing . . .
like a half nickel

*A secret cannot be kept forever. The truth
always finds a way to bubble to the surface.*

RUDOLF ABEL WAS BY ALL ACCOUNTS A BRILLIANT
man. In the 1920s and 1930s, he served as an instructor for the
Soviet Union's intelligence agency before personally leading several successful operations against the Germans during World
War II. After the war ended, he was recruited by the KGB and
promptly given the rank of colonel.

In 1948, Abel traveled to Warsaw and discarded his
Soviet credentials, replacing his identification papers with a
forged American passport. From Warsaw he made his way to
Czechoslovakia, to Switzerland, and on to Paris. In France he
secured passage on a ship and sailed to North America, dis-
embarking in Quebec, Canada. Within days he boarded a train

for Montreal, and from there, on November 17, Abel crossed into the United States.

A little more than a week later, Abel managed to acquire the birth certificate of a dead child, a forged draft card, a forged tax certificate, and—from a connection at the Soviet Consulate—more than one thousand dollars in cash. He also obtained a new passport that matched the birth certificate and, with his new identity, soon established residency in New York City.

In July 1949, Abel met with his contact from the Soviet Consulate. He was provided funding and ordered to activate a network of sleeper agents with the express purpose of smuggling America's atomic secrets into the Soviet Union.

Today, much of what Abel accomplished is still classified information. We do know, however, that during this time he was given the Order of the Red Banner, a rarely awarded Soviet medal normally reserved for high-level military personnel. He continued his work until 1957, when he was arrested for and convicted of espionage by the US federal court and then sentenced to forty-five years in prison. But he served only four years of that sentence before being exchanged for the captured American U-2 pilot, Francis Gary Powers.

How did Abel get caught? That's the best part of the story. So let's back up a bit—to the evening of June 22, 1953.

Jimmy Bozart was thirteen years old. The money he earned delivering newspapers was important to his family. They lived in a broken-down apartment with very little furniture and barely enough to eat.

On the sixth floor of a much nicer apartment building in Brooklyn lived two schoolteachers who were big tippers, regularly paying Jimmy fifty cents a week when the actual cost for their *Brooklyn Eagle* subscription was thirty-five cents. In 1953, fifteen cents was not insignificant, and Jimmy didn't get many tips that big.

That evening, Jimmy thanked the teachers and turned to navigate the six floors of stairs. At the same time, as was his habit, the boy separated the money immediately. The newspaper's money went into his left pocket. His tip money—three nickels this time—usually went into the right. But he almost missed a stair, stumbled, and dropped the coins.

The money scattered, rolling down the steps with Jimmy in pursuit. Quickly, the boy recovered forty-five of the fifty cents, but he had to search carefully for the missing nickel. He spotted it on the flight of stairs below and breathed a sigh of relief. But when Jimmy retrieved the coin, he realized there was something strange about it. What he held in his hand was only one-half of the five-cent piece.

The boy saw that it was the wafer-thin back of a Jefferson nickel—the Monticello side. Oddly, the back of the coin had detached from its front. The front, with Jefferson's profile, had come to rest several steps below. The front piece had the circular side rim, and snuggled into it was a tiny piece of microfilm.

At home, Jimmy's father inspected what his son had found with a lamp and magnifying glass but could make no sense of what he saw. The microfilm was filled with columns of numbers, each eight to ten digits long.

Jimmy had a friend at school whose father was a detective for the New York City Police Department. He took the nickel to her house and showed her what he'd found. But her father wasn't home, so he put the nickel back in his pocket and left to play stickball with some buddies.

Less than an hour later, the detective returned home and was greeted by his daughter and a fantastic story about her friend Jimmy and the nickel. Without delay he alerted his precinct captain, and within minutes the detective and other officers were scrambling to find thirteen-year-old Jimmy Bozart—and that nickel.

In case the boy had given the nickel to his mother (who had just been by the church), police impounded the bingo money. They stopped the Good Humor truck and took that money, too, thinking Jimmy might have bought an ice cream with it. Soon, however, they found the boy on the street playing ball. "You're Jimmy Bozart?" the police asked frantically, and when he answered affirmatively, they practically screamed, "What did you do with the nickel?"

Intimidated and overwhelmed, the boy simply pulled the coin out of his pocket and gave it to them. And heard not another word about it for more than four years.

In the fall of 1957, Jimmy arrived home from college to find reporters in his living room. A Soviet spy had just been arrested and identified as Colonel Rudolf Abel. Jimmy's hollow nickel had contained a coded message that was identified and read by a Soviet defector working for the Americans. The message led the authorities to Abel.

It was the smallest of mistakes, but several years earlier, the brilliant spy had mistakenly spent the fake nickel setting off a chain of events that would eventually lead to his capture.

The coin changed Jimmy's life as well. He testified at Abel's trial, and the story of the newsboy and the hollow nickel mesmerized the public. A wealthy man—a private citizen—gifted Jimmy a new Oldsmobile as a token of appreciation. A year later Jimmy received a tip from a friend that the largest sulphur deposit in history had been found in Canada. The young man sold the Oldsmobile and invested the money in a company called Texas Gulf Sulphur. The stocks soared, and at eighteen years of age, Jimmy found his financial circumstances changed dramatically.

Over the years Jimmy became an electronics manufacturer and bought several vending machine companies. He owned discos and nightclubs in New York City, a fine dining establishment in the Hamptons, and hotels, resorts, and restaurants in Florida.

The nickel remains the property of the FBI. It is occasionally available to be seen by the public, and, at a glance, it is as unremarkable as any other coin. A closer inspection, however, reveals the seam dividing the two halves. It is the smaller version of itself that holds its power and history.

It is only a half of a nickel. But it sent one man to prison and made another one rich beyond his wildest dreams.

A Little Thing . . .
like change

> *Everyone wants things to get better.*
> *No one wants things to change.*

FOR YEARS, BEFORE SPEAKING TO A GROUP, I WOULD
ask at least one of the group's leaders a simple question: What is
the most significant challenge your people face?

Overwhelmingly, the answers I received revolved around
the concept of change. Though the answers were the same, their
concerns took many forms:

- "We are dealing with change in several areas."
- "We are about to initiate some changes."
- "We are attempting to navigate a major change."
- "Several situations must change in order for us to move
forward."

- "We are just emerging from a period of uncomfortable change."
- "New regulations are forcing us to consider some changes."
- "Things aren't like they used to be."
- "The resistance to change from some areas has thrown everyone into disarray."
- "We are not getting the buy-in [from leadership, the field, clients, or someone else] that we need in order to successfully make this change."
- "Something has got to change."

(There were many more variations on the theme, but I'm sure you get the idea.)

After informing me about their challenge and its particulars, the leader usually requested that I deal specifically with the subject of change in my speech. And many of them actually told me what to say!

Over and over again I was asked to tell groups that (1) everything changes, (2) since you can't do anything about change, you might as well get used to it, and (3) everyone should read [insert title of the latest book read by the leader]. I was often instructed to add that this was the greatest book ever written about change.

For a while, I played along and did a version of what those leaders asked me to do. I walked the "party line" when it came to delivering content about change. Before too long, however, I became uneasy about the words coming out of my mouth. Not because they were someone else's words—good grief, they were *everyone* else's words—but because what I was saying seemed suspiciously inaccurate.

One day, I suddenly had an odd thought: *These things I am being asked to say could not possibly be the true answer to the challenge these people are experiencing. They have already been told what I am about to say. Their leaders have already proclaimed these "truths." Now I am being directed to say the same thing. If this were the answer, the problem would have been solved long ago.*

But the problem had not been solved. My work offered the opportunity for long discussions with the leaders of many corporations, organizations, teams, and institutions. Every conversation led me to believe that the issue of change was as debilitating—and as confusing—as ever.

For a moment, I'd like you to step outside our broader discourse and have a quiet consultation with yourself. Have you ever endured the nagging suspicion that you should be getting better results? Have you ever stopped to examine what might be missing from your efforts?

Most likely you were unable to find anything obviously wrong. So how did you respond to your conclusion? Did you simply determine that in order to increase productivity or have that breakthrough you'd sought, you would just have to work harder? Or faster? Or for a longer period of time?

You are not alone. In fact, the vast majority of ambitious people—including yours truly—have experienced the same doubts, the same search, and the same conclusions. Unfortunately, none of those conclusions proved to be the answer.

Maybe at some point, like many of us, you sighed and resigned yourself to be satisfied with the results you had always gotten. *After all*, you rationalized, *my results are pretty good. My results are better than those of my competitors.*

Or maybe, like many others, you became disillusioned with your findings and ended the endeavor completely.

Either way, your life continued. The sun rose and set. Weeks passed. Maybe months. Or years.

Until one day the unthinkable happened. You discovered that something you had believed about your work or your life was not true. You'd been lied to or misinformed. Perhaps you'd simply misunderstood. But however it happened, there was a significant piece of the puzzle you had not known about. Because you were unaware of its existence, you'd been unable to factor in a significant part of the equation—a piece that was critical to the entire process.

At that moment, you experienced the chilling realization that you could have worked forever and never achieved the result for which you were hoping . . . BECAUSE WHAT YOU BELIEVED WAS NOT TRUE.

Here's another example. Suppose we gathered in an

auditorium to witness a great physicist solve one of the most complicated questions ever posed in the history of mathematics. As the hours passed, the equation expanded, stretching from one side of the stage to the other on a giant whiteboard. We held our breath, in awe of his talent and his brilliant mind. He was, we knew, about to solve the problem while we watched.

But what if the physicist had allowed one of his students to assemble the beginnings of the equation earlier in the day? What if, in order to save time for the audience, the simpler parts had already been done, allowing the great man to work from an advanced starting point?

Now imagine for a moment that the student—way back at the beginning—had erroneously replaced an x with a y. Just a simple mistake, but the resulting frustration suffered by the physicist would be immense. For despite his IQ and expertise, he would be unable to successfully complete the problem.

In fact, the man could work until the end of time, and it wouldn't change the outcome. The problem could *never* be correctly solved . . . BECAUSE THE PHYSICIST BELIEVED SOMETHING THAT WAS NOT TRUE.

The concept of change doesn't seem nearly as complicated as a mathematical equation, does it? If it *isn't* complicated, why are we so consistently confused by change? Why does it give us such a hard time?

For one thing, change is a constant and all-encompassing reality. Change is a part of everything we do, every day of our lives.

Think about it. You grew up. Things changed. You became engaged. Things changed. You got married. Things *really* changed. You had problems in your marriage? Obviously, things changed. You wanted to get your relationship back on track? Of course, but some things had to change. And on and on.

In languages and dialects the world over, there is no term or expression used to designate another foundational reality that affects so many parts of our lives. There is not another single word on the planet that comes close to describing the *power* of CHANGE.

But if change is such a familiar part of our lives, why are we so consistently confused and upset by it? Why does it give us such a hard time?

Simply put, it has to do with *what we believe* about change.

Curiously, there are three things.

These three basic beliefs have been taught and talked about so often and for so long that they have been accepted as fact, are never questioned, and have now become a part of our societal consciousness. They influence the economy, our government, our work, and our relationships.

These three things we believe about change are so fully ingrained into our daily lives that they play a major role in every decision we face.

Through the decades, we have gradually made cornerstones

of these three beliefs. We treat them as principles, using them to determine how we lead, what we expect, and when it might happen. These beliefs quite literally dictate what society accepts as possible or impossible in terms of human behavior.

Given all the books that have been written and the speeches that have been made, all the courses that have been taught and our almost universal acceptance of these beliefs as unassailable facts, can you even imagine the frustration we might experience if just one of these three beliefs was shown to be a bit off-kilter or even wholly incorrect?

Well, considering the books that have been written and the speeches that have been made, taking into account the courses that have been taught and our almost universal acceptance of these beliefs as unassailable facts, what are the odds that *all three of them* would be utterly and absolutely wrong?

Impossible, you say? Read on.

MYTH #1: IT TAKES TIME TO CHANGE.

There are many variations of this fable: "Change is a process." "Change is slow moving." And so on. But they all revolve around the central misconception that it takes time to change.

Allow me to put it this way: no, it does not.

Change happens in a heartbeat. In the snap of a finger. In the blink of an eye. It may take time to *prepare* to change. It may take time to *decide* to change. But true change, when it occurs, happens instantaneously.

MYTH #2: A PERSON MUST
WANT TO CHANGE.

Most of us have believed this for years. It seems so rational that we never considered its veracity. In fact, we take that conviction even further and assert that, oftentimes, a deep desire is required for true and lasting change.

A brief examination of events in our own lives, however, will quickly convince us that this is not remotely true. In fact, you and I could spend five minutes together and come up with any number of personal stories to illustrate the many times we've made lasting changes without any previous desire to do so.

Consider the occasions in your life when everything was moving in a particular direction. Your relationships and career seemed stable and on their usual course. At a particular moment, however, you acquired new information. That new information may have been opportune or it may have been tragic. But at that very moment, you changed, moved in a different direction, and never looked back.

In that instance, you had no "want" or deep desire to change. Until that moment, you didn't even know the possibility of change was on the horizon! Yet a true and lasting change was made. And it happened in a heartbeat.

MYTH #3: A PERSON WON'T CHANGE
UNTIL HE HITS ROCK BOTTOM.

How many times have you heard the "rock bottom" thing? It goes something like this:

> Well, you can try to help again if you want to, but the reality is that he is *not* going to change until he hits rock bottom. We thought he was at the bottom. He may have thought he was at the bottom, too, but he obviously wasn't. A person just does not get that deep desire to change until they really are at rock bottom.

Sorry, this one's not true either. It sounds good and is believed so universally that it's practically a cliché. It's just verifiably inaccurate.

Surely you have known someone who was in and out of drug or alcohol rehab so many times that the family finally had said, "No more!" and refused to finance another stay in the clinic. You might not have seen this person for years until, one day, you ran into him quite by accident. To your astonishment, he appeared to be happy, healthy, and prosperous. In answer to your congratulations and questions, he related a story of how, after years of struggle, he had met a person and had a conversation—or had read a magazine article or seen a television program or gone to a church. "That very day," he professed, "I went home and poured everything down the sink and have not wanted it since."

Or perhaps you know a person who had smoked for decades, never able to quit until, one day, he declared, "Several months ago, I had a conversation with a coworker. That afternoon I went home and threw my cigarettes away. Since that day, I've not had a single one."

So what is happening? What planets have somehow aligned when a person—well above rock bottom and without a deep desire to change—actually changes dramatically in an instant? Which pieces of what unknown puzzle must be in place in order for that change to be lasting and real?

There are only two.

Before I reveal the two pieces of the puzzle that must be in place in order for real change to occur, allow me to confess that I have been quietly testing this assertion for several years. During the past eighteen months, I have been teaching it from the stage. As I explain the (apparently) unfailing power for change these two pieces provide, I also issue a statement, followed by a challenge, to the audience. Here is the statement:

During the past several years, I have intensely examined two specific elements that seem always to be in place when true change occurs. I am aware that *always* is a strong word. However, after studying individuals, small groups, organizations, corporations, and teams on a local, regional, and national basis, I have been unable to find a single example of real change in which these two components were not present.

And here is the challenge, given to audiences of corporate executives, parents, coaches, ministers, married couples, politicians, sales staffs, and students:

If you can find just one example of true and lasting change that does not contain these two things, I would love to hear about it.

As of this writing, neither I nor anyone else has found that example. Evidently the combination of these two ingredients for true change is without exception, for its record continues to be perfect.

CHANGE INGREDIENT #1: WHAT'S IN IT FOR ME?

This component is not an expression of greed or selfishness. It's just an outgrowth of the normal desire for self-preservation that exists in every human being. Whether it is expressed aloud or not, when a person is asked (encouraged, prodded, ordered) to change, this is the thought process that is triggered:

> Well, I've been doing it this way, and I know you want me to do it that way, but if I do it that way, how does it affect me?

And if we were really honest about our private musings, we'd have to admit they sometimes continue along like this:

> Me—that's what I think about most often. I can't help it. I don't talk about it because I know how it sounds, but I'm on my own mind a lot.
>
> I love my family more than me, but to make a living for

them, I have to think about me because I am the one who does the work. I have to plan and prepare myself, and how can I do that without thinking about me?

Flight attendants tell me to place the oxygen mask over my own face before helping others—even small children. Doesn't that mean I must first think about me?

It's a struggle to admit to these kinds of thoughts. You and I value humility so greatly that uncovering this subconscious thought process can be alarming. But it helps to understand that to think of "me" includes those we love and the people or things for which we are responsible. So "What's in it for me?" also means "What's in it for my company, for my family, for my team, for my neighbors, and for my nation?"

In this context, there's nothing wrong with considering "me." And the truth is, there can be no true and lasting change in any arena if this element is not addressed.

An easy example that most of us have experienced in one way or another is that of a teenager whose behavior a parent is attempting to change.

First, it is important for the parent to identify what kind of change is desired. If it is change for only a season that the parent is after, then punishments and threats may well do the trick. If you want your teenager not to talk a certain way or wear a type of clothing and to respect you as long as he or she is in your house, you can make that happen. I will admit that it's a constant fight, but it is relatively easy to pull off. As long as the teen *is* in your house, you can probably make him or her do whatever you want. After all, you are bigger than your teenager, and you have all the money.

But if you're wanting true and lasting change, that is not likely to happen with demands for respect and threats of grounding or speeches that begin with, "As long as you're in my house . . ." If it is true and lasting change a parent is after, you must remember that the teenager won't always be in your house.

Consider the statement "You will not talk to me that way." Or "I am your father, and you will respect me." Both are somewhat enforceable in the short term, but if true and lasting change is what the parent desires, you must note that neither statement has "anything in it" for the teenager.

So, you ask, if a parent desires a teenager to speak respectfully or dress in a certain manner, what could possibly be in that for the teenager? I promise to fully answer that question after revealing the other half of the puzzle.

CHANGE INGREDIENT #2: PROOF BEYOND A REASONABLE DOUBT

Proof is an essential component of change for the simple reason that, to a thinking person, anything proven to be true is unassailable. If you believe one thing and the opposite is proven to be true, you immediately change what you believe. Forever.

Are you tempted to go back to what you believed before? Do you waver back and forth? Of course not! You were given proof.

Not opinion. Not several correct options from which to choose. Proof. And that proof cemented what you now know as fact. It also showed in no uncertain terms that what you previously believed was incorrect.

Proof trumps uncertainty. Proof leads. We might question motives. We often question conclusions. We question methods and timing. But we do not question proof.

As we face great change and turn to assess a new direction, the journey often appears to be entirely uphill. Without proof, we are often beaten before we start, for doubt can be an overpowering foe. Only proof stands as a knight in shining armor astride a white stallion at the top of the slope, beckoning us onward and upward. And as we surge to the summit—across doubt and through fear—we do not have to deal with uncertainty about our mission or anxiety about our course. For there, right in front of us, is proof.

It is important to note that this proof, required as an element of change, does not have to meet the standards of a mathematical proof. Remember, this is proof *beyond a reasonable doubt*. Or evidence strong enough to convince.

Proof beyond a reasonable doubt, when offered and accepted, sometimes takes a person aback. It raises eyebrows and drops jaws. When confronted by proof beyond a reasonable doubt, people think, or even say out loud, things like this:

- "Well, that makes total sense."
- "I never considered that."

- "I can't believe that never occurred to me, but it's true."
- "Gosh, I'll never again think about this any other way."
- "I'm going to have to rethink some other things now."

Let's continue the example of changing a teenager's behavior in a true and lasting way. Consider for a moment the teenager who reacts to guidance from a parent by rolling his eyes, sighing loudly, and saying, "I know, I know, I know!" As we discussed earlier, the parent might demand respect, shout, and threaten, but none of those options will be effective in the long run because none offers anything in it for the teen.

In the same way, there is not a shred of proof in those responses either—unless you count the certainty of trouble and strife "as long as you are in my house." There's nothing there to convince the teen to choose a different way, nothing to show *why* a different approach would be better. There's no proof—just a power struggle, which the teen knows the parent will win. Is the relationship deepened? Is there a newfound respect from the teen because the parent demanded it? Or is there more determination by the teenager to simply endure until he or she *is* out of the house? The bottom-line question is this: Even if the teenager does not roll his eyes in the presence of the parent again, has true and lasting change really taken place?

Consider the following—a real explanation, after an incident like the one just described, offered by a father to his fourteen-year-old son:

You know, I can understand you being tired of hearing me talk. Sometimes I get tired of hearing myself talk. So give me three minutes, and I won't talk anymore . . . for now.

Okay, here goes. I was thinking about our conversation last week about the car you want to buy when you're sixteen, the things you want to do. You even told me what you wanted your life to be like when you were twenty-five. I was impressed. I want you to be able to accomplish everything you listed. I really want to help too. Sometimes I think I want you to have that awesome life almost more than you want it for yourself. But obviously, I can't create that life for you. I also know that I can't force you to do the things that will get you there.

Now, I suppose I could make you dress a certain way or talk a certain way for a while. After all, right now, I'm bigger than you are, and I have all the money! But I'm at least smart enough to know that when you are away from me—and definitely when you are old enough to move away permanently—you will do whatever you want to do anyway.

So even though I want the very best for you, I cannot make it happen. You have to do that. But I keep asking myself, *I love this kid so much . . . how can I help?* All the things I have nagged you about in the past—how you act, what you say, how you say it, what you wear—while those issues might cause me some short-term aggravation, what I really want is to be able to explain to you *why* your mom and I try to steer you in certain ways.

You may have assumed that we want you to act a certain way because of our standards. And you may think that those things don't really matter in the long run because your standards are different from ours. Again, I am at least smart enough to know that you will choose your own standards anyway, so none of it is about our feelings or our control or authority or anything like that. It is *all* about you. It is all about helping you live exactly the life you want to live. I want you to accomplish everything you desire.

Here's what I mean. Obviously, I don't think you should roll your eyes and say "I know, I know, I know" to your mom or me or any adult. But here's *WHY*: It looks and sounds incredibly disrespectful. And you are not a disrespectful person. Therefore, I don't think you want other adults to hear or see you acting that way. After seeing or hearing you do that—or, get this, even hearing about it from someone else—they might conclude that you are a disrespectful person.

Because they believe you are a disrespectful person, you will not be hired. Not by them or any of their acquaintances. Because they believe you are a disrespectful person, you will not be given the opportunity. And it continues from there. Potential clients never even consider you or your business. You don't get the letter of recommendation you need. You are not invited, you're not allowed to date their daughters, you aren't chosen to . . . [deep breath] we could go on and on, right?

In any case, there are a thousand things that people who

are perceived as disrespectful never have the opportunity to do or become. And the worst part is that they never even know why they weren't chosen or included.

Okay, I'm through. You don't need to respond to any of this now. Or ever. Just think about what you really want out of life, right now and as an adult. Maybe this will help.

About an hour after the father's explanation, he and his wife (the young man's mother) received a heartfelt apology from the teenager. In addition, the sincere expression of regret was delivered with a spirit of gratefulness. The young man communicated his appreciation for the patience his parents had demonstrated. He expressed amazement at his new level of understanding. And to his dad, he added, "Thanks for not knocking my block off for acting like a jerk."

Several years have passed since that incident. According to the boy's father and mother, there has never been another incident in which that son acted disrespectfully. Not one.

Somehow, at the age of fourteen, that young man experienced a true and lasting change. That change did not "take time." It was not a change for which the teenager was longing. He had no deep desire to change. And while there was a moment of family disharmony that prompted the father to initiate a significant change, it is safe to say that none of the principles described in this story was anywhere close to "rock bottom."

So what happened? First, it is important to note that the father was not shooting in the dark. He knew a change in behavior was needed, and he went after that change with confidence. Because of earlier conversations with his teenager, he was quite familiar with his son's hopes, dreams, and desires. He knew what kind of car the boy was working to buy for himself when he turned sixteen. He knew where and in what manner the teenager wanted to live in eleven years, at the age of twenty-five.

With this knowledge, it was a fairly simple task for the dad to demonstrate how closely aligned the granting or withholding of life's opportunities is to how a person acts. By pointing out the obvious necessity of opportunity to one who desires accomplishment, he quickly covered the first element required for change.

In other words, the father communicated to his son what was in it for him if he changed his behavior.

The second element required for change—proof beyond a reasonable doubt—was fulfilled by illustrating how people of influence react to disrespectful behavior. It made total sense to the teenager. He saw the truth (the proof) in his father's illustration immediately. For a moment, he imagined himself as a person of influence in a position to help someone with an opportunity. Would he give the opportunity to a sour, impatient, disrespectful teenager? Nope. He knew—not suspected, but KNEW—that his father was correct.

At that moment, what was in it for him collided with proof beyond a reasonable doubt. And the change he experienced was instantaneous and lasting.

Change will probably always be a challenge in your life. It's human nature to resist it. But if you understand the myths and the elements of change, you can respond to it with confidence and creativity and even joy. You can help others respond positively too. Change can be initiated on your say-so and on the timetable you set. Change can be navigated with precision. Change can be directed.

Say a corporate buyer always purchases widgets from a certain vendor, and you want that buyer to purchase his widgets from you. In other words, you need that corporate buyer to change. So you arrange a meeting and prepare to state your case, which can be done in many different ways. But if you can demonstrate to that buyer what's in it for him (and his company) and if you can prove beyond a reasonable doubt that this is so, then the likelihood is great that the buyer will change vendors. You will have been the agent of that change.

If a neighborhood rule needs to change, all the arguing in the world will not do the trick. But if you can show what's in it for your neighbors and illustrate proof beyond a reasonable doubt that it is so, the rule will change.

In any form, with any person or group, the principles hold. When what's in it for them aligns itself with the truth and reality of proof, change is the inevitable outcome.

Change is such a little thing. But as far as little things go, not a single one has bigger ramifications. Change is not our enemy.

It needn't confuse or bewilder us. Properly understood, change can be a medium of peace and harmony.

"How?" you ask.

Well, if the change you initiate is responsible, there really will be something in it for the person or group you are asking to change. And if the proof is really there—knowing that proof is truth—there need not be prolonged arguments.

In regard to our families, our businesses, and society as a whole, if you and I can learn to initiate changes based on value and truth, we will see everything change.

This is how you and I can change the world.

✒ Fourteen ✑

A Little Thing . . .
like the best

> *Good will always be the enemy of best.*

IF YOU COULD CHOOSE, WHAT KIND OF LIFE WOULD you live? Where? How? With whom? What would you do to create value for other people? Whom would you mentor? Who would mentor you? What would you discover or learn? How would your understanding change things for the rest of us? What would you leave for your children and grandchildren? What would you want engraved on your statue when this life is over?

Has anyone ever asked you questions like these before? Yes, of course they have. In speeches, books, sermons, and classrooms, most of us have heard these questions or others like them. Most of us even answered them. From that point, however, we never gave the questions *or* the answers another thought.

Read the first sentence of this chapter again. Do you see the trap? Do you see why so many of us are indifferent to the question and completely disregard the answers—our own answers?

No? Look again. Look at the first four words. It is there that the danger exists.

It all seems so harmless and fun, a little game of "What if" just like we played as children. But we are not children, and the wording is not harmless. Naive perhaps, but not harmless.

Try vile, deceitful, and destructive. Why? Because those four words and the way they have been posed to you since you were a child have slyly informed you over and over again that life itself is a roll of the dice. Like most of us, you have been casually convinced—slowly conditioned to believe—that you have no say in the matter.

Do you see it now? Those first four words—*if you could choose*—have been used by egomaniacs and tyrants throughout history to mentally and physically enslave entire populations. That's because the words impose a belief that is stronger than shackles and chains.

The principle is little known but heartbreakingly true: it is impossible for a person to outperform his acknowledged capability.

Or, stated another way, a person cannot achieve beyond what he really believes to be the truth about himself.

Put yet another way, this principle states that what a person really believes is so powerful that his belief actually controls his behavior.

In fact, to correctly predict the level to which a person might achieve, one needs only to discover the truth about what that person believes. (Please note: This principle has nothing to do with whether what a person believes is actually true. It's simply about the connection between that person's limits and what he truly believes deep in his heart and mind.)

Incidentally, this is why many people do not hit the goals they set. After the balloons and excitement of New Year's Day or the somewhat forced process of goal-setting at work, they don't really believe they can achieve what they wrote down on paper or publicly proclaimed to their friends. Therefore, it doesn't matter what their goals might be. They can write pages and pages or glue colorful words on a poster or put sticky notes all over their bathroom mirrors and affirmations on their phones. But deep in their guts, if they don't *really believe* what they have stated as goals can be accomplished, you can rest assured they won't be.

Rabbit Trail Alert! Same Topic, Different Application

Merge onto this pathway to cement your understanding.

Or quietly skip the following twenty-nine paragraphs and continue reading on the main road.

For some years, I have had the privilege of working in an unusual role supporting some of America's defense personnel. I have been flown in F-16s, B-1s, B-2 Spirits, Pave Lows, Pave

Hawks, and modified C-130 gunships—both the Spooky and Spectre. And yes, I shot the guns.

Twice I successfully completed a Special Operations anti-terrorism course. More than twice I've been awakened in the middle of the night by different three- and four-star generals requesting an understanding or a methodology for modification of performance behaviors. Once I even spent Thanksgiving overseas in a field hospital with some of our wounded soldiers. The relationships I continue to enjoy with leadership and certain Special Tactics personnel within the US Special Operations Command and our intelligence services have been particularly rewarding. And wildly interesting.

Generally, the men and women in these areas of service are just like you and me. Generally. If there is an apparent difference, it is usually a difference of degree or intensity.

For example, you and I exhibit a certain level of self-discipline. Most of them—again, generally speaking—exhibit more.

You and I prize humility. Often they practice humility to the point of lifelong secrecy.

You and I adhere to a strong work ethic. Their work ethic is so far off the charts it can't even be categorized by mortals like us.

You and I are loyal to our friends. These men and women are loyal not only to their friends but also to the friends of their friends—people they don't even know. Sometimes they prove that loyalty by dying.

Here, though, is perhaps the biggest difference I have identified:

You and I (hopefully) are open to new ideas. But Special Tactics personnel are open to new ideas on an entirely different level. These people—including the intelligence services—actively seek new ways of thinking as passionately as a treasure hunter might dig for King Solomon's gold.

Oh, and they seem to like sports. And since I have worked with a number of head coaches, managers, general managers, and captains of teams in various sports, I have a number of stories I can relate to clients and friends. My wife would say that the specific number of stories in my arsenal is "a lot." In any case, they are fun to tell, and most of them teach one point or another.

One evening, in a secured location, our specific tasks were completed for the day. I was with several general officers and their aides. Dinner was finished, and as we relaxed, we entertained one another with stories. Before long, the stories began to revolve around the theme of leading people and helping an individual or team perform beyond their level of ability.

During the course of the evening, I related several experiences I'd had with college football teams, one from Major League Baseball, and a couple more from professional golf. Each tale revolved around the mental aspect of performance, and soon our conversation had turned to the subject of belief.

As we talked, someone remarked that belief is such a powerful force that it could probably be weaponized. With the utterance of that word, *weaponized*, the eight or ten folks in the room came to full alert, and we began to probe the possibility.

I told the story of Lewis and Clark and what they had

accomplished with the Girandoni air rifle (see chapter 10). I labeled Lewis's tactic as "belief imposition"—deliberately influencing what the Indians believed about the rifle. Then, for more than an hour, we explored, shaped, and began to describe—hypothetically—how this "weapon" might function.

These professionals were intensely aware that an opportunity was before us. When life and death quite literally hangs in the balance between certainty and hesitation, even the smallest tactical advantage can tip the scales. Such an advantage can be on par with new weaponry or new technology when it comes to decreasing casualties and increasing the level of safety and confidence for intelligence operatives undercover or spec ops teams on the ground.

So everyone in that room was steely eyed and fully alert during this discussion, sensing that an opportunity lay before us—an opportunity that inspired us to shove against the heavy boundaries of what we already knew to be true.

At one point, I spoke slowly, thinking through a possibility for utilizing belief imposition as a fighting strategy. "Okay . . . what people believe determines their behavior, right? This is a fact. But think about this: what people believe will determine their behavior *whether or not what they believe is true.*"

I paused before continuing as we mentally cemented that strange but accurate thought into place. "So if we wish an enemy to behave differently—perhaps in a fashion his rational mind has never previously allowed—it is the enemy's belief system that we must attack.

"Think of it this way: If we want the enemy to do a certain thing—move to another location, for instance, or act in a specific manner—then we must cause him to believe something that has never occurred to him before. Or we must convince him that something he has always known to be a fact is now no longer valid. If we can find a way to shift or change what the enemy knows to be true—to impose a specific belief upon him—it will be a relatively simple thing to influence his behavior and direct his actions."

At the time, there was a concern in these circles about vulnerability in a specific piece of body armor. Reminding them of that issue, I said, "Look, you've already seen evidence that the enemy knows to target that particular place, right?" They nodded reluctantly. "Well, think about it this way," I continued. "If somehow the enemy became absolutely convinced that Luke Skywalker or Captain Kirk had outfitted our teams with invisible, impenetrable shields that covered that part of their bodies, then . . ." I raised my eyebrows.

"If an enemy absolutely believed it, he wouldn't even try to shoot our guys there. The conclusions we'd convince him to make would not be true, but they would still determine his behavior!" Everyone chuckled thoughtfully, and for a few minutes we tossed around some beliefs that might actually be imposed in order to guide and, in turn, predict an enemy's behavior.

You might be interested to know that I have taken the concept of belief imposition into several collegiate and professional sporting situations. The results have been exactly as you might imagine. The playing field—or the court or the course—is just as susceptible to this tactic as any other arena in life. In almost any kind of endeavor, absolute belief controls behavior absolutely. In fact, there are so many variations on this theme that an entire book could be written listing successful examples. So without admitting to anything or naming names, allow me to illustrate a way belief imposition might be put to work.

If you've attended a game—NCAA or NFL—you already understand why the home crowd is urged to "make some noise" when the visiting team's offense is on the field. Especially on third downs. The quarterback calls a snap count that his linemen must hear. If they can't hear it or if they aren't sure the voice they're hearing is that of their leader—both of which can happen easily when the crowd is noisy—mistakes become more likely. And those errors lead to costly penalties or missed blocks.

In most stadiums the crowd takes very seriously its responsibility to disrupt the opposing team's communication with as much noise as they can muster during critical moments in the game. But some fan bases are better at it than others. There are those who say the Seattle Seahawks fans have turned noise-making into an art form. Screaming at the top of their voices and stomping as hard as they can with their feet, all the while using their hands to operate whatever device they can find that makes a racket, the Seahawk faithful consistently push the sound meter above 130 decibels. And in case you are interested, 130 decibels—according to comparative analysis produced by the Federal Interagency Committee on Noise—is equal to being fifty feet away from the tail end of an F/A-18 Hornet as it leaves an aircraft carrier. On afterburner.

While teams are allowed only eleven players on the field at a time, enthusiastic Seattle supporters have become such an effective "twelfth man" that in 1984, Seahawks management actually retired the number 12 jersey in their honor. The noise they create continues to have a drastic effect on opponents. On November 27, 2005, the New York Giants had eleven false-start penalties and missed three field goals in a loss to Seattle—all because of the crowd. The next day head coach Mike Holmgren dedicated the game ball to the fans—the Seahawks's twelfth man.

Now, suppose for a moment that you and I want to help a football coach mitigate the noise at an opposing stadium famous for it. With the game a whole week away, we might suggest some lines for the coach to sprinkle into his press conferences and newspaper interviews, his weekly radio show, and his weekly television program.

Anytime the topic of hostile crowd noise is broached, the coach will reference new technology created for his team or a new system of communication they've just adopted. He will be cagy about it, of course, bringing up the topic of his break-through only when asked about stadium noise. And because the upcoming opponent's fans are famous for their stadium noise, he *will* be asked.

At some point, the coach might smile mysteriously and say, "Well, you know, they can scream their heads off if they want to, but it won't really matter to us." Then he'll chuckle and add,

"Maybe I shouldn't say anything 'cause *now* it's kind of funny to us, but we've got it covered. The noise is just not something we even talk about in team meetings anymore. It is no longer a factor for us."

After those statements, the interviewer will naturally begin to push for more details. And the coach will be instructed to laugh good-naturedly and say, "Nooo . . . I've probably said too much already. I don't need to talk about this anymore!"

From that moment, word will begin to filter through news sources and talk shows, and by the time the game rolls around, a significant number of the fans will have concluded that any noise they might make will now serve no purpose. So they don't make it. And the decibel rate at that game is reduced by forty points.

Remember, nothing changed but what the crowd believed. Because they believed they had been rendered powerless, they didn't even use their power. And the opposing team was able to hear the quarterback's signals with no problem.

A few months ago, several years after the impromptu meeting with the generals, I had an unexpected encounter with one of the men who had been in the room that evening. In an out-of-the-way place he'd arranged, the man told me that he had commanded several military operations since that time, including one that made news all over the world.

He removed a gift from his pocket and presented it to me. "I've been holding this for you." My eyes widened. "Remember the conversation that night?" he asked slyly. "Well, I wanted you to know that belief imposition has been an integral part of the success of these operations. Especially in *this* one."

I was stunned, of course, but thrilled—and reminded once again how much of a difference a little thing can make. In this case, it had been a tiny shift in thinking.

Incidentally, this same man has been rewarded for his successes with additional responsibilities. He is currently based overseas, serving our country and its allies. Recently awarded an additional star, he capably commands an unusually focused and gifted group of people.

After our meal not long ago, I put down my iced tea, looked him in the eye, and asked, "What . . . I mean exactly *what* . . . are you doing now?"

His smile was easy but careful, and he shrugged. At the same time his hand drifted into the air, and he moved or shook it around as if he didn't know exactly where to put it. And he said, "Oh, you know. Just a bunch of little things."

Notice: This Rabbit Trail Has Officially Ended

Please Continue on the Main Road Below

Hmm, where was I? Oh, I remember! I was closing in on PROOF of the value of *understanding* a little thing called THE BEST.

For the moment, though, let's go back to the first four words of this chapter: *if you could choose.*

Four words—subtle but, at the same time, daring. We have seen, heard, and spoken those four words so often through the years that we never even considered pausing to contemplate their veracity. Pull back the curtain, however, and you'll quickly see the truth.

Those four words—IF YOU COULD CHOOSE—stand like a dangerous politician in a three-thousand-dollar suit. Leaning comfortably on the podium, flashing a dazzling but sincere smile—pearly white porcelain caps, his face framed by a haircut a doctor couldn't afford. Tanned and lotioned, gesturing with manicured hands to emphasize the honeyed baritone of his glorious voice, he is lying through his teeth. And we are lapping up every word.

"If you could choose"—that seemingly innocent beginning of a game or lead-in to a conversation has subconsciously suborned the vast majority of us into achieving far less than we might otherwise have accomplished. In plain English: Forget about the fact that we have *not* experienced THE BEST life has to offer. Most of us have never even allowed ourselves to consider what THE BEST might actually be!

> ***Special note:*** I apologize to you, dear reader, that I was
> not able to place a dump truck load of exclamation
> marks at the end of that last sentence. My editors

were probably honors English students in high school.
I was not. They certainly know their way around
sentence diagrams better than I (better than me?
myself? us?). And they have consistently informed me
that I use entirely too many exclamation marks.

In addition, they do not like it one little bit when I use various-sized letters, when I change fonts in the middle of a sentence or (God forbid!) when I **bold** or *italicize* certain words. And as you've seen, I did it anyway through much of this book. Neither do they approve of my occasionally beginning sentences with the words *but* or *and*. But I do it anyway. And as several of my books have reached bestseller status, I claim this as my style.

Regarding the exclamation marks, I continue to argue that the reader is reading a book. That means I cannot raise my voice to exhibit the importance of a particular sentence. Neither can I underline the words with a cheap ballpoint pen strongly enough to get the reader's attention with a rip in the paper. Alas, that leaves me with only the literary garbage of an exclamation mark or two in my dimwitted arsenal for conveying the significance I wish to place on those words.

Obviously, any arguments offered by a bozo like me to editors as scholarly as the ones in charge of my books have always been to no avail. That being the case, allow me to add here that if I *could* have written the sentence like I wanted, I would have written it this way:

Forget about the fact that we have NOT experienced THE BEST life has to offer. **Most of us have never even allowed ourselves to consider what THE BEST might actually be!!!!!!!!!!!!!!!!!!!!!!!**

All that to say, the first four words in this chapter are a dirty, rotten lie.

BECAUSE YOU *CAN* CHOOSE.

You probably did your best imagining before the age of seven. Somewhere along the way, however, you learned the "truth" about your future. You would not be an astronaut or a movie star. The older you got, the more aware you probably became about this truth. Because your possibilities seemed less likely, your aim sank even lower.

You believed every limiting thing you heard, read, or suspected about yourself. And in the meantime, you just got on with life. True, life was not incredible, but it wasn't horrible either. The world in which you lived was merely a statistical reality. "Look around," you told yourself. "Be happy with what *is*. Why should I be different? Why should I long for something more or something else? Why shouldn't I be happy with the way things are? Things are fine."

And things *were* fine. They weren't great, but they were fine.

You did what you were supposed to do. You achieved— perhaps not at the highest level, but on whatever scale of joy, contentment, and prosperity everyone else was measured by, you were definitely higher and better and more than some others. Statistically, you were miles away from lowest and worst.

And remember? You were okay with it all. You really were. You believed life was supposed to be that way. Because everything you believed about yourself and your life was . . . true.

It was *all* true.

But maybe, just *maybe*—maybe it was all true because that's as much as you could manage to believe.

Look around you. Right now, look around.

Is there anyone else in the room? If there is, and you are at home, casually close the book and slip out. Go somewhere else. Or if no one is there, stay where you are. The point is to find a quiet place for you and me to talk privately. So if you have to go somewhere else in order for us to be alone, do it.

Go. Go now. I'll wait.

Okay. Just you and me, right? No one is reading over your shoulder? Good.

Now, may I ask you a personal question?

Yes?

Okay, take a deep breath and give me an honest answer: Do you believe in God?

No, wait. Not so fast. Think about it. Think hard for at least a second or two.

Do you *really* believe in God?

I am aware that if I manage to convince a hundred people to read this book, the truly honest answers to my question will be all over the map, up and down the scale, from one extreme to the other. From yes to no, with every degree and variation in between. There will be those who stop reading here, offended that I even mentioned God. And there will be those who write scathing reviews (with lots of misspelled words) on the Internet, outraged because I didn't mention God on every page.

Here, however, for a brief moment, you have been granted an increasingly rare chance encounter with someone you might not know as well as you think. And I'm not talking about me here. Right now, wherever you are, you have the opportunity to think *for* yourself while you are *by* yourself. To ask yourself some questions. And to answer them all for yourself.

It's quiet. You are alone. Settle in.

Now, here's the question again: Do you believe in a God who is here, now, with you? A God of the universe who loves you and cares about you and wants THE BEST for you?

If your answer is somewhere south of a yes—if you aren't sure—I would urge you to quietly but urgently continue searching for that answer. Find a friend who is certain of his or her yes and ask for direction. I'm quite sure that your friend or someone your friend knows can answer your questions and lead you to a confident and joyful place.

If, however, your answer is already affirmative, then I have just three more things for you to think through.

So you are a *yes*.

Yes, you believe in a loving God who cares about you and wants THE BEST for you?

Okay, good. Me too.

The second thing I want to ask is a little odd, but here goes: Do you think God has a better imagination than you do?

You're a *yes* on that? Yep. Again, me too.

All right. Then here's the last question—and it's a game changer, I think. Are you ready? Take a deep breath and think with me now.

If you believe God wants THE BEST for you . . .

And you know that *you* obviously want THE BEST for you . . .

And you *also* believe God has a better imagination than you . . .

Then when we examine your life—the life you declare to be THE BEST you can imagine—and we place it alongside your life that is THE BEST *God* can imagine . . .

IS IT POSSIBLE THESE TWO LIVES MIGHT LOOK ENTIRELY DIFFERENT?

Have you ever laid out an opportunity with the possibility of great rewards for someone you loved—or perhaps more than one someone? As you watched them struggle, you quietly prayed for them, hoping beyond hope for their success. Without interfering, you closed your eyes, tensing, using every fiber in your being in an attempt to will them onward and upward. And then, after hanging in there for a while and accomplishing a certain amount, these people you loved—perhaps even your own child—just stopped trying. They didn't actually quit. They just hit a certain mark, maintained their position, and happily accepted whatever rewards were available for that level of effort.

If you have been in this position—or if you can imagine it—you know how much it can hurt. For a parent, it is anguish to know a child could have *had* more, could have *become* more, could have gone farther and higher if he or she had only looked up. Had only kept going. Had only believed what you said was possible!

Tragically, you realize that you wanted that greater outcome—THE BEST—for your child more than your child actually wanted it for him- or herself. You knew your child's capabilities. You knew what it would take to reach the prize. You knew there was a joyous end to the struggle. But he or she didn't believe it. And now, every time you look at him or her, you think of what could have been.

What *should* have been.

Knowing that God is our Father in the purest sense of the word, we surely know he loves his children at least as much as we do ours. I wonder how he feels watching us. Does he sometimes shake his head in despair? Does he think us weak or dense because we refuse to see purpose in the struggles we are allowed to face? When we refuse to even try?

Greatness is never a product of frailty. Physical and emotional and spiritual muscle is only developed through struggle, and with that muscle comes increased ability and newfound strength. Capacity, competence, and wisdom grow as they are exercised against the resistance of things considered impossible for now. The muscles developed during difficult times are what will eventually turn impossibilities into achievable opportunities for the future.

The inevitable conclusion . . . the only reasonable reality . . . the foundational truth . . . the bottom of the pool is this: You and I should spend less time setting goals to satisfy the expectations of other people and use *more* time to concentrate fully upon legitimately increasing the level of what we really and truly believe is possible. This can only be done—it will only ever be done—by aligning ourselves on a course to pursue the life that God himself has identified for us as the very best.

I'm curious. Aren't you? What might he have in mind?

A Little Thing . . .
like opening our eyes to what is already there

Perspective is how we decide to see a thing.
Blindness is the decision not to see it at all.
Choosing a negative perspective is limiting,
but choosing blindness is a tragedy.

MY FAMILY LIVES IN A GREAT NEIGHBORHOOD. WE know our neighbors and often visit one another's homes. We've lived here for what now seems like a long time. In fact, it's the only house our boys have ever known.

If you've read my novels *The Noticer* and *The Noticer Returns*, you know my story. For a time as a young man, I was homeless. During the day, I worked odd jobs and roamed the beach. Nights were sometimes passed in empty garages or, most often, in a place I had hollowed out where the concrete met the sand underneath the Gulf State Park Pier. I still drive by that huge structure several times a week. It's only six miles from my house, but in many regards, it's a world away from where I live today.

One afternoon last December, my wife, Polly, and I left home about fifteen minutes before dark. We were headed an hour away to meet some friends for dinner. At the stop sign marking the exit from our neighborhood, we faced the usual two options—the *only* options if one is driving. With the beach and the broad expanse of the Gulf of Mexico directly ahead— due south—our choice was either left or right. East or west.

Our friends lived in Gulf Breeze, a destination that required a left turn, but Polly and I looked longingly to the right. It wasn't that we were unsure of our directions.

"You can just see that it will be great, can't you?" my wife murmured as she reached for her phone. "The sky is getting ready to show off." She fumbled with the icons on the phone's screen, locating the camera and adding playfully, "I wish we were eating with the Bullards tonight."

I smiled, nodding in agreement. It was no reflection on our friends in Gulf Breeze. The Bullards—Joe and Foncie—lived in Point Clear, near Fairhope, on Mobile Bay. Driving to the Bullards's would have allowed us to turn right, heading directly west. And though the sunset had not even begun, experience told us that the clouds and the reflection of the Gulf waters would make this evening a sight to behold . . . for anyone driving west.

"Oh, well," I sighed. And with a last glance to the right, we turned left and headed east.

Fifteen minutes later I had almost forgotten the sunset Polly had predicted when she looked over her shoulder and gasped. Quickly she snapped a photograph with her phone. "Look," she said and placed the phone up and into my line of sight. A quick glance, and my eyes registered the photo she had taken. I had seen it for less than a second, but that was enough to make me shake my head in wonder. The photo she had taken with her cell phone—the one I had seen so briefly—had captured the surging crimson of a blazing sky.

Indicating the phone with a tilt of my head, I said, "That photo is unreal. It's incredible—even though it obviously doesn't compare with the real thing." I jabbed my thumb behind us, asking, "So what's the real thing like back there now?" Traffic was heavy on the two-lane road, and I didn't dare turn around to look.

"Unbelievable," she said. "Totally different from two minutes ago but still unbelievable. Maybe more unbelievable." Polly played with her phone for a moment before sliding toward me as far as the seatbelt would allow and turning her whole body in order to keep watch behind us. As she rested her chin on the seat back, her dark hair brushed my shoulder. I breathed deeply, catching a trace of her perfume.

Polly was quiet as she stared out the rear window. "If you wanted," she said teasingly, "you could turn the car around, put it in reverse, and back all the way to Gulf Breeze." I smiled at her comment but didn't respond. Instead, I reached to hold her hand and continued to concentrate on the driving, paying close attention to the taillights in front of me and the headlights of the other vehicles passing us on the left.

As I drove, my wife kept up a running commentary, describing the slow explosions of intensity and fusing color as the heavens shifted and moved, bursting with an effort that looked as if the sky believed it would never have another chance to create a sunset.

At last Polly sighed, the sound revealing a unique combination of excitement and satisfaction. It was almost completely dark now, and the spectacle had faded. Still, as Polly turned to face forward, she continued to talk about the swirls of color and moving clouds, attempting to describe for me what had made the sunset so magnificent.

Listening to my wife as we drove along, I realized I wasn't too disappointed, having missed it. For those of us who live along the Gulf Coast, a sky like the one that evening is practically commonplace. Not that we get tired of them, but fabulous sunsets are not exactly rare.

"I've never thought of this before," Polly said suddenly, "but in a way I almost envy the time in your life when you lived on the beach, sleeping under the pier." After a moment, when I hadn't responded, she added, "You know?"

I remained quiet until she lightly swatted my leg. "Dear, did you hear me?"

"Umm . . . I did," I answered haltingly. "I'm just trying to figure out why you would envy any part of that."

"Well, I was thinking about you being outside on the beach

every evening, listening to the surf. I was thinking about how many sunsets you got to see."

Again I was quiet, and once more, after a moment, Polly spoke. "Hey, dear, are you listening? What are you thinking about?"

"I was thinking about that time, just trying to remember . . . and you know what?" I glanced her way quickly, making sure *she* was listening. "Maybe things really have changed since then— the atmosphere or whatever. Because . . . ahhh . . . well, we didn't have these brilliant sunsets. Not with all these colors. Actually, as I think about it . . . well, there just weren't any. Not like now, anyway. I mean, now—good grief, there are beautiful sunsets several times a week *now*. But I gotta say, I almost never saw one back then, and I was on the beach every evening.

"Strange," I concluded. "That has never really occurred to me."

For a time we drove in silence. I sensed the unsettling edges of sadness creeping over me, and I wasn't sure why. But scenes from my past, featuring a much younger version of myself, flared uninvited into my mind. I remembered how, sometimes as early as noon, I would begin to dread the end of the day. The fear was a physical presence, a fist increasing its grip in my chest as every clock I managed to glimpse moved steadily toward dusk—the time to find an empty garage for a few hours or crawl under the pier, alone for the night.

I've never forgotten the heaviness of the humid air on those late afternoons so long ago as the daylight I imagined to be "safety" transitioned to evening and a gradual quieting of the beach. The last winds of the day were dying, and the tourists were leaving the beach for air-conditioned hotel rooms, showers, dinner with their families, and beds—real beds with clean sheets. The stillness left behind was ominous to me, alone, as the evening faded into night. The darkness was an enemy, both literal and figurative, an oppressive predator that overwhelmed my conscious mind before I could get to sleep and attacked me with nightmares as soon as I did.

"Dear?" Polly spoke softly and reached across to briefly touch my arm.

"Hey," I responded, blinking and straightening in my seat. Noting quickly where we were on the drive and realizing my wife had noticed my "absence," I smiled and reached over to give her a pat. "You good?"

Her eyebrows lifted a bit. "Yes," she said. "What about you?"

"Me?" I replied. "I'm fine."

Polly nodded. "What're you thinking about so hard?"

"Oh, you know. Nothing. Everything. Just general stuff."

She nodded again, remarking, "That didn't seem to be a 'thinking about general stuff' look on your face."

Without anything to say at that point, I said nothing and was relieved that Polly didn't pursue the subject. After a while, our usual casual conversation started again. We talked about the boys, about a friend whose mother was sick, and about a football coach I had talked to earlier that day.

After a bit I noticed Polly had her phone and was quickly

scanning through the screens. "What're you looking for?" I asked.

"Something I want to show you," she said. "Hang on. You'll like this." Moments later, after apparently finding what she was searching for, Polly looked up. "Can you pull over—just for a minute?"

I didn't ask why. A parking lot appeared to our right, and I turned in. As soon as the car was in Park, Polly smiled mysteriously and began to speak. "When the sun was going down, I took some other pictures while we were talking. Look at this one," she said, turning the camera to face me. "This is my favorite. I took it before I turned around."

I stared at the image on her phone, immediately deciding that, yes, it really was more incredible than the first photo she had shown me earlier—maybe more incredible than any sunset I'd ever seen.

"Do you see what I did?" she asked.

I smiled and nodded. "Wow" was the only thing that came to mind. The way she had taken the photo made it even more stunning. (To see this stunning sunset, go to AndyAndrews.com /Sunset.)

"I took it in the side mirror," she said.

"It's awesome."

Polly waited, allowing me to study the image closely and send it to my own phone. Polly was quiet until I handed it back. Then she turned it toward me again. "It's not really a photograph of the sunset, you know."

I frowned. "What?"

"Look at it," she said, and I did. "It's a photograph of the passenger-side mirror on a car."

My eyes narrowed. "Okay . . ."

She smiled innocently. "I just thought it was interesting. I was facing forward when I took it, you know? The truth is that I only saw the mirror. At that moment, I never laid eyes on the actual sunset. But it was back there. See?" She shoved the phone's image toward me again.

"I see," I said carefully. "And what does that have—"

"Hang on," Polly interrupted. "Here comes the really interesting part. I turned around and watched the rest of the sunset. I even took pictures. But you didn't turn around. I know you were busy. You were driving. But the fact remains: you never once turned around to look. You did *not* see it."

My wife was staring at me expectantly, but when she didn't say more, I looked at my watch. "We need to go, don't we?"

Polly slowly smiled. "We do," she said, "but . . . I want to say this again . . ."

My eyes were wide. I was trying hard to mask my impatience. "Okay," I said simply.

She took my hand. "Dear. This evening the sky was as beautiful as it's ever been. In reality, you never saw the sunset at all. Not once. But you know what? It was there whether you saw it or not. It was right behind you the whole time."

Today, I don't mind admitting to you that we had almost arrived for dinner before I finally hit upon what Polly was trying to tell me. Her lesson, however, has stayed with me ever since.

True, more than three decades have passed since I lived on the beach, but there were just as many sunsets then as there are now. The fact that my self-pity and anger allowed me an excuse to ignore beauty—to choose blindness—does not mean that sunsets did not exist at that time.

Surely there were sunrises as well. And rainbows and full moons and stars scattered across the night sky like a vast black canopy, inset with a million diamonds and lit from behind. And I missed it all.

Again, it is important to note that for a time in my life, I *chose* to be blind. Because of that choice, I was blind not only to beauty; I also was blind to opportunity, to forgiveness, to the value in others, and a host of other things, material and spiritual. My rejection of these virtues at that time effectively neutralized any chance I might have had to pull myself into the light of a better life.

Please be aware: a person who obstinately chooses blindness is a dangerous step or two beyond mere pessimistic perspective. A gloomy way of seeing things is only a walk along an unguarded cliff. Choosing not to see the cliff at all, however, can be the end of everything.

To be clear, perspective is how we decide to perceive a thing. Blindness is the decision not to see it at all.

Choosing a negative perspective is limiting.

Choosing blindness is a tragedy.

As you and I navigate the rest of our lives and help others understand how to successfully navigate their own, we must be aware that opening our hearts and minds to reality is a necessary part of being able to live each day with proper perspective.

In other words, we must choose to see before having the opportunity to choose how we see it.

Not the Conclusion . . .
because the little things are only the beginning!

SUPPOSE FOR A MOMENT THAT SIDES ARE BEING CHO-
SEN for a game that will last a lifetime. The object of the contest
is for one team to out-achieve the other, personally and professionally. Each group is allowed one player from any time period
in history—a great mind whose thinking will guide the others.

As captain of Team One, you are awarded the first pick.
Who will you choose—Aristotle or Einstein? It sounds like a
tough decision, I know, but it's really not. No, not at all.

Go with Einstein.

"Whoa, now—wait a minute," you're probably saying. "There's
no way!" Furthermore, if you are familiar with Einsteinian logic,
you might well believe that by suggesting Albert I have rendered this entire book irrelevant. "After all," you could assert,
"Aristotle is the one who went 'small picture.' Einstein moved in
exactly the opposite direction! Einstein was a big-picture guy if
ever there was one!" And, of course, you'd be correct—at least
your point about Einstein being a big-picture guy.

Confused? Don't be. Fortunately, as in so many situations, a closer examination reveals greater understanding.

Consider it from this angle: While it is true that Aristotelian logic is "small picture," the reason is, it moves thought in that direction. Aristotelian logic is a form of reductionism. As it moves to the smaller picture, it quite naturally shrinks and excludes.

Einsteinian logic, on the other hand, does move toward the big picture. Einsteinian logic is nonlinear, and as it moves thought toward the larger view, it quite naturally grows and includes.

After all this time together, surely you are not surprised that I want big things for you. Our very reason for examining the *little things* in the first place was to give you a more complete understanding of a foundation upon which you can build a large life of ever-increasing opportunity.

You were not made to bury yourself in minutia of constantly decreasing size. Your life has been created for growth and inclusion. It is intended that you use little things as a springboard or a pathway to the big picture (i.e., masterpiece) you are making of your life. The little things are simply the means we employ to achieve the end result we desire.

Sadly, most people will probably continue to grab for a big picture without ever establishing a firm foundation. Most people will never understand that the little things are only a beginning point, but that without a proper beginning point, growth is greatly inhibited. Most people, like the mockingbird, will sing the same song as an adult that they sang in their youth. In other words, left alone, most people tend not to change very much.

Most people are threatened by new information. Why? Because new information requires us to remap our minds, and sometimes that includes changing what we believe.

Most people don't understand the struggle to understand, nor do most people *want* to. This lack of understanding, coupled with a lack of desire to grow, ensures that most people never reach so much as the outside edge of the potential in their lives.

It is sad but true. For most people, what they know for sure is yesterday's news.

So let me say this: *thank God you aren't "most people"!*

You are prepared. And continuing to prepare. You have already learned so much, and you are hungry to learn more. You are curious, delighted by wisdom, and willing to interest others in the pathway you have chosen. Your pathway is one of joy. It is filled with excitement and ever-increasing reward because you have chosen to be generous with all you have received.

If I had a magic wand I could wave over you, I would declare your eyes wide open, for the time has come for you to make use of what you know to be true and share with others the person you have become. I would declare your mind, soul, and spirit open as well. With my magic wand, I would have you live a life so valuable and rewarding that only God's hand could begin to explain it all. I would proclaim yours a family of rare wisdom and financial abundance as the joy, peace, and influence of your legacy echoes through generations.

Unfortunately, you and I both know I don't have a magic wand. *Fortunately*, that fact matters not in the slightest. Magic wands are like four-leaf clovers, shiny pennies, and rabbits' feet, and neither you nor I need any of them.

Luck is a myth. Luck is undetectable because it is nonexistent. Luck is something wished for as the dice are rolling and blamed as soon as they stop. Luck is called upon for mercy, grace, peace, and abundance by those who do not have anyone else in their lives upon whom they can call.

You don't need luck. You are strong, smart, and capable. You will choose wisely because you have already chosen to open your mind, soul, and spirit to the vital little things and their promise of ever-bigger things to come. You are gaining understanding. You are becoming more valuable every day. And soon you will have the peace, influence, and obvious results to prove it.

So from me to you, congratulations in advance for the life you are about to lead—a life so rewarding that only God's imagination can provide the blueprint.

A Reader's Guide

INTRODUCTION

1. How could an adjustment in perspective make a significant difference in your personal life or career?
2. How could you make use of the benefits of being a "Noticer"?
3. Andy Andrews is a *professional* Noticer. Do you think this is simply because he thinks differently from most people, or do you think this kind of discernment is a gift? Why?
4. Have you created any masterpieces lately? Why or why not? If so, why did you do it, and how did you do it?

AUTHOR'S NOTE

1. Andy hopes that as you have read this book, it has prompted you to think differently. What do you hope to have gained by having read it?

CHAPTER ONE

1. In many circumstances, we wouldn't think of the number *one* as being a powerful number. What is the important significance of *one*, and what can make it so powerful?
2. Often the gap between numbers *one* and *two* is wide. What causes this gap? How and why does this happen?

CHAPTER TWO

1. Andy states that there is a big difference between "history" and "the past." What instances can you remember that demonstrate this difference?
2. Why do we omit so many tiny details if it truly is *the little things* that really count?
3. The Battle of Waterloo was impacted by a fistful of nails. Do you know of other significant historical events when something that seemed so small made such a big difference?

CHAPTER THREE

1. Andy shared a story about a new school in Utah that chose the cougar as its mascot. The local school board refused to allow the cougar to be the new mascot because "the word has a derogatory connotation and *might be offensive to older women*." Is this an example of going overboard with political correctness, or do you think the school board made a fair

decision in this instance? Can you think of other examples in your local community or state where something like this has happened? Did you support or oppose the decision? Why?

2. Explain what the term "tail wagging the dog" means. What examples of this can you name that are apparent to you in today's world?

3. Is there such a thing as absolute truth, or is truth a situational concept that depends on the situation at a particular moment? In your opinion, how do most people perceive truth today—as an absolute or as a situational concept?

4. What is the "butterfly effect"? While the butterfly effect often produces amazingly positive results, what kind of catastrophic problems could the butterfly effect present by people who are offended and angry within a family or a community?

5. Do you believe that you have the ability to "choose how you act, despite how you feel," and that you are in "total control" of choosing to be offended about something or not? Have you ever been offended? Are you holding on to this offense? Do you realize the danger in this? What can you do to overcome it?

CHAPTER FOUR

1. Do you think our society today underestimates the power of the little word WHY? Do you think it's a valuable question that deserves to be explored and answered? Why?

2. When things are going well, most people don't think to ask WHY. Why is this the perfect time to ask yourself, WHY?

3. In chapter 4, Andy has a fascinating way of describing the different types, or groups, of people who exist in our world (the zs, $\mathcal{D}$s, $\mathcal{T}$s, $\mathcal{L}$s, $\mathcal{H}$s, and the off-the-chart $\mathcal{W}$s). In which group would you place yourself? Which group do you aspire to be more like and why? What will you need to do to make this happen?

4. We learn in this chapter that "principles are the most valuable form of common sense." While living by certain principles is a good thing, and knowing HOW these principles work is essential, it's not until we ask WHY they work that we actually will be able to apply those principles to all areas of our lives. Are you fully aware of the principles that govern your life? Can you name them, and do you know WHY they actually work? How is this affecting your daily life at home, at work, or in your community?

Chapter Five

1. We often hear people celebrating the time they *almost* reached a goal or *almost* accomplished a major life event. Is this really a time for celebration? What is the significance of one-sixteenth of an inch or two degrees where *almost* could become a very dangerous concept?

2. Do you ever get discouraged when you begin a new project and things aren't going quite as quickly or smoothly as you

had imagined? How does that discouragement affect you physically? Is it debilitating for you? What advice does Andy give us for turning this situation around and pursuing our dreams once again?

CHAPTER SIX

1. Andy's dad taught him a tough lesson about quitting. When is it okay to consider quitting as an option, or is it ever okay? Why?

2. Andy's dad knew that quitting was not a practice with which Andy wanted to become comfortable. Do you think our society, in general, has become very comfortable with the process of quitting and giving up too easily? If so, what do you see as the result of this? If not, why do you think people persist when life gets tough?

CHAPTER SEVEN

1. Do you agree that we interpret the facts incorrectly sometimes? Do you ever do this? Can you think of an instance when this could be dangerous?

2. Have you ever changed your thinking about something? Did it significantly affect anything? What is the value in examining and re-examining your thinking?

CHAPTER EIGHT

1. Socrates, Aristotle, and Plato were all great thinkers from a long time ago. Who do you consider to be the great thinkers of today? What makes them so? How are they different from most people?

2. Why do people refuse to challenge the thinkers of today? Should we challenge them? Why?

3. When does a person "arrive at the finish line of learning"? Have you arrived there yet? How do you know?

4. Andy makes the following statement in chapter 8: "A little more understanding can change the world." What does that mean to you?

5. When you are ready and willing to examine your own thinking, Andy says that you will need to ask yourself some serious questions. What questions can you come up with that will make a difference in your life?

CHAPTER NINE

1. Chapter 9 begins with the following quote: "Perspective is the only thing consistently more valuable than the answer itself." Why is perspective so powerful?

2. Do you really choose your perspective? What shapes these choices about your perspective? What is the relationship between *perception* and *perspective*?

3. Perspective can really affect the decisions we make, but

timing is an extremely important factor as well. What is the main difference between the way most people arrive at their decisions and the way wise people make their decisions? How can this knowledge help you in making your decisions?

4. Consider the contrast between the decisions McDonald's and Chick-fil-A made about being open on Sundays. You would think that being open extra days and hours would result in more profit, but in this case, it clearly does not. What do you think has contributed to Chick-fil-A's overwhelming success in spite of being open fewer days and fewer hours each year than McDonald's?

Chapter Ten

5. In chapter 10, we learn the remarkable story about Meriwether Lewis and the power of one air rifle. Was the rifle that powerful, or was it Lewis's incredible marksman skills, or was it something else even more powerful than either of those that protected his party from attack? Perhaps it was the known versus the unknown. What do you think, and how was this possible? How could you use this knowledge to help you succeed?

Chapter Eleven

1. "Everybody wants to make a difference, but nobody is willing to be different." In what ways do you see this manifested in today's world?

2. The phrase "average excellence" seems like an oxymoron. What do you think about it? Do you or most of your acquaintances and friends fit into that category? Why or why not?

3. Most teenagers don't have a desire to be different from their peers; they want to blend in or fit in with everyone else. Do you find that most adults struggle with this same feeling? Why or why not?

4. How does one become comfortable with being different? What is the difference between being weird and being different? How can we inspire or encourage others to be different?

Chapter Twelve

1. How did one nickel, actually half of a nickel, become so valuable to Jimmy Bozart and have such a tremendous effect on his life and his future?

2. In this case, the truth eventually caught up with Rudolf Abel. Have you ever discovered that someone was giving you false information? Do you believe that the truth is always found out? Why?

Chapter Thirteen

1. Why do people often resist change? What changes have you resisted? Why? Is change always a bad thing?

2. Andy mentions that change affects many parts of our lives and that it's very difficult even to describe the power of

change. Describe how you or someone you know has been affected by change. Was it powerful? Why?

3. Our nation has been through quite a few changes during the last several years. How have these changes affected our country and its citizens? How powerful were these changes? How might they have affected other countries and the way they view America?

4. Andy says there are three basic beliefs most people have about change and that they influence every decision we face. He goes on to say that all three of these beliefs are "utterly and absolutely wrong" and continues by explaining why they are myths. Name an instance in the past when you realized something you believed was simply untrue. How did that awakening affect your life?

5. Andy firmly believes that there are only two "ingredients" that must be in place before real change can occur. As you read more about these two ingredients, how do they concur with or change your view about change? How will this help you when dealing with family and coworkers who are having difficulty with changes you are trying to implement?

CHAPTER FOURTEEN

1. How can "belief imposition" work for you at work, within your family, and with friends?

2. Have you ever really considered what THE BEST might actually be? We all want what is best for us, best for our

families, and best for our careers, but what exactly does that look like? How would you describe THE BEST?

3. Now, here's the real challenge that Andy gives us: Examine your life (the one that seems to be THE BEST you can imagine). Now place it alongside THE BEST life God has planned for you. How do you think they would compare? Are there any similarities at all, or are they vastly different? What can you do to get those two more closely aligned? Why would you want them to be more closely aligned?

4. We've often heard that during times of grave difficulty, we develop great strength—the kind of strength that defies all odds and enables us to become overcomers. Where does this kind of strength come from, and how will it serve us in the future?

Chapter Fifteen

1. Polly reminded Andy that the sunset was there whether he saw it or not. How does that translate into something you might have chosen not to see?

2. According to Andy, our "perspective is how we decide to perceive a thing. Blindness is the decision not to see it at all." Have you ever asked yourself how some people could be so clueless or so blind to the things going on all around them? Is it because they choose to see it from a perspective that is clearly different from your own, or is it simply because they choose not to see it at all? How can you make a difference in

the lives of others who choose blindness or, perhaps, need a perspective adjustment?

NOT THE CONCLUSION

1. Why would Andy choose Einstein to be on his team? Whom would you pick and why?
2. Many people believe in luck. Andy says it is nonexistent—a myth. What do you believe about luck? Why?
3. How has this book affected your thinking? How will it affect your choices, your perspective, and your decisions? What will you do differently from this day forward? How will this affect your life and the lives of those around you?

About the Author

HAILED BY A *NEW YORK TIMES* REPORTER AS "SOMEONE who has quietly become one of the most influential people in America," Andy Andrews is a bestselling novelist, speaker, and consultant for some of the world's most successful teams, largest corporations, and fastest-growing organizations. He also personally coaches individuals and small business owners to become Unshakeable Entrepreneurs at AndyAndrews.com. He has spoken at the request of four United States presidents and recently addressed members of Congress and their spouses. Zig Ziglar said, "Andy Andrews is the best speaker I have ever seen." Andy is the author of the *New York Times* bestsellers *The Noticer*, *How Do You Kill 11 Million People?*, and the modern classic *The Traveler's Gift*—which has sold millions of copies worldwide. He lives in Orange Beach, Alabama, with his wife, Polly, and their two sons.

CONTACT ANDY

To book Andy for corporate events, visit

ANDYANDREWS.COM

OR CALL

800-726-ANDY (2639)